LIFE IS BEST LIVED

Simple Lessons from Life

By Dr. Carroll Marr

xulon PRESS

Life is Best Lived
Simple Lessons from Life
by Carroll D. Marr

Printed in the United States of America

ISBN 9781619046627

Unless otherwise indicated, Bible quotations are taken from The New American Standard version. Copyright © 1999 by Zondervan.

www.xulonpress.com

Dedication

I must dedicate this book to my father Earl Marr and mother Loma Marr for the love, patience, and compassion they demonstrated as I grew up. Their commitments to Christ and godly lives were a true inspiration. I am grateful that they provided an environment where a young boy could learn that "life is best lived." I must also express appreciation to my Tanya for her loving support in every endeavor I have attempted throughout our life together, and finally, to my sons who have been a lasting source of joy and a true blessing to my life.

Thanks

I must offer a special thanks to my assistant, Julie Locke, for her help in putting this together and her creative input on titles. She is a true gift. I wish to also thank Amy Everett for reviewing the manuscript and offering her editorial skills.

To you, the reader, who might take the time to actually read these stories, I hope they are a blessing to you.

FORWARD

I grew up in a privileged time. A time when children could set out for adventures without parents giving thought to abductions by sexual predators. Dangers existed, but for some reason were nominalized, allowing a child freedom that has, since that time, become unknown. It was a time of innocence and simplicity. No computers, internet, cell phones or pagers - we didn't even have "colored" TV. And the black and white set we had received only three channels. It was a simpler time but one that afforded children freedom to play and roam and use their imagination.

I also grew up in a privileged environment. My home was a happy one where a mom and dad loved each other and their children. We were a family given to basic Biblical morals, the kind this society was built on. This privileged environment was also a rural setting. Rural America in those days provided the perfect background for a childhood rich with opportunity and adventure.

It is from this privileged background that the stories in this book find their origin. They are true, though in present times may appear to be something of a Norman Rockwell painting. I am blessed to have lived in this window of time. You will see why.

Chapter One

Garden Arrowhead

My dad grew up in a large family, the son of a share cropper. That meant his dad farmed another person's land and paid rent by giving the landowner one-half of the crop. Share croppers in that day were generally poor, and it was hard work. Dad and all his brothers and sisters did their part to help the family survive. From a young age, Dad would plow ground with a team of mules. I have heard many stories of those years, each told with a sense of nostalgia.

When I was around six years old, Dad pastored a small church where an older member owned a mule. He and Dad decided to raise a large garden together, and Dad used his mule to break and prepare the land. By this time, mules were something of a novelty since it was rare to see someone actually plowing with one. I was fascinated by the whole ordeal and was not alone in my interest. It was common for people to drive by, turn around, come back and stop just to get a closer look. Old men would stop and relive their own childhood experiences. Some would return with their children or grandchildren. It became quite a spectacle. For a six year old, it was just fun.

I still remember the plow as it rolled the dirt like ocean waves breaking against the shore and the smell of fresh plowed ground. From start to finish, I experienced farming the old fashioned way. Mr. Griffin, the old gentleman who owned the mule, was too old to offer much help, but his presence at the end of the garden, heavy-set, faded overalls and cane looked like a Norman Rockwall painting.

The thoughts of that spring and summer still linger vividly in my memory. I still have a piece of that memory – a tangible memento that, when held, brings me back there. Back to the sounds of the click my dad made from the side of his mouth as he urged the mule forward, the "whoa!" at the end of the row that brought the massive animal to a stop. The command "gee" or "haw" that, to a mule, means left and right. The smell of rich soil and the joy of being a boy in a fun place. All of these sweet memories wash over me when I hold a simple treasure I found in that field and kept all these years. The sharp clink sound from the plow as it slipped through the dirt indicated that something irregular just beneath the surface had been unearthed. I dug the tilled ground to reveal a small arrowhead, the first of many I would collect through the years. This one is different, though. It transports me through time and space to a garden spot in my childhood.

It is amazing how our memories can become connected to tangible objects. Perhaps that is why God would so often instruct the nation of Israel to build a memorial to the events He wanted them to remember. This was often nothing more than twelve stones arranged in a pile. Yet the sight of the stones was enough to spark a question from a child and, consequently, spur the retelling of the event.

What tangible reminders do you have that bring to mind a childhood memory? It could be as simple as a stone or a photograph. Take a moment to relive a memory of joy from your childhood.

Chapter Two

The Middle Biscuit

My mother prepared a home cooked breakfast every day during my early childhood. That was before microwaves and the pre-packaged stuff. I enjoyed the real thing: eggs, bacon, grits and home-made biscuits. As an adult, I understand the effort that went into those meals, but at the time, it was just breakfast.

Along with the normal eggs and bacon was the homemade pure cane syrup our neighbors made. At some point in my elementary years I developed a love for syrup and whole cream, mixed together and eaten with a biscuit. In our health conscious world, the mere thought of it makes my heart pump harder to push life through what must be cholesterol-lined veins. But in those days, food did not cause such problems.

For several weeks I settled into a routine of pouring syrup then cream and then taking the middle biscuit and mashing it into the mixture. The memory alone is almost more than I can take. That was as some country boys say, "Slap your Mama good!"

Now, the recipe for perfection required the middle biscuit, and everyone knew this. Yet, equipped with that general knowledge, my brother sat down for breakfast one morning just as I put the finishing touches on the syrup and cream mixture and took the middle biscuit! Despite my immediate and passionate exception, Dad ruled that my brother should get it, besides no one was going without - there were other biscuits on the table. But, this recipe specifically required the middle biscuit. From that moment on, the war raged. If I got the middle biscuit – as I should, given the recipe - my brother would protest. If he got it, then I would protest. After several miserable mornings, we sat down to breakfast and discovered my mother had prepared a pan of biscuits that had two in the middle! Neither of us wanted one.

Funny, how we are often drawn to the forbidden, or long for what we cannot have. It is human nature, because our nature is sinful. The desire for the forbidden fruit leads us to believe that the fruit we can have does not compare to the one we cannot. Somehow we think God must be keeping the best from us or He would not forbid our having it. The lure of sin always leads us to believe that it is better than what we have. Time and time again we take the fruit and make the stark discovery that it is not as good as what we had. But that memory fades quickly and when faced with another forbidden opportunity, we must have it. I think the struggle is solved by looking at God and not the forbidden fruit. When one understands God's amazing love for us, one can understand that He would never keep the best from us; He offers us the best. We see the one tree God said to leave alone and miss the entire forest of trees He provides that offer the best available. God is a loving God who directs our path and gives His word so we can know the best life has to offer. He is not trying to keep us from the best but, instead, give us the best. The answer to the dilemma is to trust the heart of the Father; if God says it is bad, it is and should be avoided. He is not trying to keep you from that which is good. My mother wanted me to have the best she could offer and wanted the same for my brother. If the best was the middle biscuit, she found a way to give one to both of us. The scripture says, "If our parents being by nature evil know how to give good gifts to us, give us the best they can, how much more will our Father in heaven give good things to us" (Matt.7:11 my paraphrase). You can trust Him.

From the day of that conflict forward, my mom fixed biscuits with two in the middle, but for some silly reason I did not think they tasted the same. They did of course, but a selfish attitude can put a bad taste in your mouth.

Chapter Three

Thunder

When I was in the third grade, my dad discovered a "what-a-deal." A "what-a-deal" is Mississippi for a bargain. A man in our community had a Shetland pony complete with bridle, blanket, and saddle for the handsome price of $20. Thinking this would be a great deal for me, he bought him. Thunder was a beautiful black pony with a rather shaggy coat.

We built a stall for him behind our house and introduced him to his new home. He was an extremely gentle pony, but as I painfully discovered, had a fond propensity toward biting. I think the only thing he liked more than biting was to bite with the dramatic element of surprise. When you least expected it, Thunder would quietly approach from the rear and then promptly perform the "bite and run."

If you have never been bitten by a horse, words are not adequate to describe the pain; if you have, no words are necessary. Thunder introduced me to the very fine line between love and hate. I loved him, but each bite brought with it an intense hatred for this animal.

Come to find out, biting was not his only vice. It seemed that Thunder was not fond of being ridden and was quite adept at unloading his cargo. His gentle nature kept him from bucking, thus the strong "No." offered by the previous owner when asked if he bucked. At the time, we did not know to ask if he bit, and full disclosure was not required by law when buying ponies. Though he never bucked, he had discovered other, more effective, ways of unloading unsuspecting third graders.

His favorite unloading method was connected to his love for biting; he would simply turn his head, grab the rider's pants leg or bare leg and pull him off. This method was most effective and normally rendered the rider unable to return to the saddle. If the rider became aware of this tactic and performed counter measures, he would then move toward any inanimate object such as a tree, house, barn, car, etc. and would scrape the rider off. His final tool, and one he had perfected, was to run at full gallop, and just as the rider began to enjoy the Lone Ranger moment, slide to an abrupt halt while putting his head down. So, the rider would roll over the front. With the rider in a humiliating pile before him, he would then return to the barn and wait for round two.

Over time I became quite good at the counter and evasive moves necessary to ride Thunder, but it was never enjoyable. I guess I learned at a young age that not every deal is as good as it looks. It took a while, but we were able to unload, I mean sell, the horse and tack for $20, even though my dad insisted on full disclosure. When I argued this full disclosure thing was not necessary, he took a moment to teach me about true character. "The truth will set you free." he said. "Tell the truth and no man can accuse you of being dishonest." Honesty and character stuff was a big deal to my dad. His generation coined the phrase, "A man's word is his bond." It was his generation that would seal a deal with a handshake and believed that a man was as good as his word. Perhaps Tom Brokaw was correct, this was the greatest generation. It seems to me the greatness came from a commitment to the principles of God's word. It is interesting that many of the people who held to these principles were not religious or even Christians, but the impact of the biblical principles was the same. Our nation was founded on the principles of God's word and the closer we move toward her founding, the more we see the overwhelming influence of those biblical principles. If we ever hope to see character make a comeback that will permeate through society, it will be the result of a return to those foundations illustrated in God's word. Character is a good word, even if you are stuck with Thunder the Biting Horse longer than you desire.

Chapter Four

Powerful Pet

One day a neighbor offered my dad a baby raccoon. Heavy rains had caused some local flooding, and a mother raccoon moved her kittens into our neighbor's barn and left them there. We took one and named him Racky. Baby raccoons are a lot like cats and kittens. They are both born with their eyes closed and do not open them for several weeks. We received Racky early enough that he quickly became accustomed to us and, since we fed him with a bottle, assumed we were his family.

Raccoons are by nature inquisitive creatures, and Racky was no exception. They are also nocturnal so Racky slept most of the day and ran around the house at night. He was very playful and smart. He also loved sweets, most particularly syrup. One Wednesday evening before church, Mother prepared a breakfast menu for our dinner - eggs, bacon, biscuits and syrup. After our meal, we walked to church for the regular Wednesday night activities and returned home about an hour and a half later. When we entered through the kitchen door, we discovered that Racky had found the syrup pitcher Mom had left on the table and helped himself. He actually climbed into the pitcher head first, and all that was sticking out was his tail.

Racky was an unusual pet, and in spite of his mischievous nature, he was fun. But his greatest value to me was connected to the extreme fear my friend Benny had of him. The discovery of this weakness in Benny's life soon became a guaranteed method of getting my way.

Carroll: "Let's play cowboys and Indians."

Benny: "No, I want to play army." Carroll: "I'm going to get the coon."

Benny: "No! I want to play cowboys and Indians."

Carroll: "Yipee Kiyay!"

It seems that fear was a powerful motivator. In fact, often the Bible says we should fear God, and that can be confusing. Is the scripture saying that we are to be afraid of God, to see Him as an angry God on a throne with a lightning bolt in His hand looking for the opportunity to zap us? That is the way some see it. On the other hand, some believe He is a buddy. I have heard people refer to Him as the man upstairs. But this is a dangerous position. To fear God is to have a reverential awe. He is God, creator, sustainer, sovereign ruler of the universe. He is our father, He is loving and merciful, but He is still God and demands our reverential respect. To fear Him is to know who He is and, from that understanding, realize that I must never do anything that would dishonor or disregard Him. To live in fear of God is to live aware of His presence and power.

And in light of that, one who fears God lives to fulfill those purposes. I am not scared of God. He loves me and would never do anything that is not for my best. He can be trusted. He is faithful, but He is at the same time, God. When He speaks I must listen - He is God. When He tells me what to do I have no choice, He is God. To fear Him is to honor Him as God and to yield to His command.

Chapter Five

Smell the Truth

One summer my dad preached a revival at a small country church about an hour from where we lived. We often accompanied him to these revival meetings. My mother and brother would sing during the worshiping time. I went ... well, because there was no one to baby-sit. Generally, I did not like attending these revivals, but this week was different.

The pastor of the church where Dad was to preach had a son my age. The first night of the revival, we were to arrive early and eat supper with the pastor's family before attending church. I was particularly excited about this since it would provide an opportunity to hang out with this pastor's son. We knew each other but rarely had opportunity to spend time together.

They lived on a small farm, and we walked around outside as the final preparations for supper were being accomplished. As we walked around the barn, my friend said, "We have a hog big enough to ride." Naturally I asked to see, and he led me to the back of the barn and to a small square pen that contained the largest hog I had ever seen. Intrigued, I asked if he had ever ridden the animal. "Yes," he replied, "all the time." I then began to focus on details, "How do you do it?" My friend then explained that one of us would need to get into the pen, and as the hog ran from us around the side of the pen, the other would wait on top of the fence. When the hog raced by, we would simply jump down onto him. Realizing that I might never have another opportunity to ride a hog, I told my friend I wanted a ride.

The perimeter within the pen was mostly dry, but the middle was muddy, allowing the hog a cool place to wallow between rides. I asked about the muddy part of the pen and was assured by the resident expert that the hog would stay to the dry, outer edge. With this assurance, I positioned myself and, with perfect timing, mounted the giant hog as he ran by. I rode the beast for at least two rounds before a graceful dismount. It was amazing – really! I am numbered among the few men who have ridden a hog. One of the only ones you may know who has done so.

I brushed the dirt off just in time to hear the call to supper, and we headed home. As we entered the back door, we were greeted by the adults who were covering their faces with their hands demanding to know, "Where have you boys been?! You smell awful!" I thought that because there was no evidence of mud on my clothing, no one would know. Evidently, there is a smell associated with hogs that will linger even after parting ways. There is a great lesson here. Sometimes the influence of wrong company can make its way into our lives without notice – at least to us.

Jesus said, "Cast not your pearls before swine." (KJV Matthew 7:6) In other words, don't give what is valuable to pigs. They could never appreciate it. Be careful who you hang out with. Their influence could be a lasting one. Their influence might not be a visible one, but it is influence none the less and will become apparent somewhere along the way.

Chapter Six

To the Dump

" To the Dump:" may evoke the thought of a trash truck taking the garbage to a land filed, but in my childhood days it meant a trip to a nearby ravine where the locals would dump trash. There is an old saying, "One man's trash is another man's treasure," and that is certainly the truth for boys looking to decorate or expand a fort.

Fort building was a major part of my young life. Boys have a deep understanding of their role as Protectors of the Universe and know that a well-executed attack can come at any moment. Forts are essential for national security. The dump was a wealthy source of the essentials in fort construction, and I am convinced that their absence in our day has created a shortage and a breach in our national security. (Our nation was never attacked on my watch, we were ready.)

Our adventures to the dump put us in direct contact with germs and filth unspeakable, but it was a simpler time and no one noticed. We went with parent's full knowledge, cautioned only to watch for broken glass.

More than germs and disease, the dump served as a breeding ground for a boy's imagination and creative genius. An old bedframe would become a wall for the new expansion, an old car seat became a new sofa, an old dresser provided wood to connect all the pieces. The key is to look with new eyes. Look at what can be, not what is. It is all about potential. At the dump we were looking for what an object could be - not what it currently was.

This ability, if mastered, can provide a perspective that will lead you to a new adventure in life. Seeing with new eyes, not what has been but what can be, is God's perspective. He views us in light of potential that we and others around us may not see. When Jesus first called Peter, He used this "perspective" to see beyond the fisherman before Him to the great leader he would become. "You are Simon," He declared, "but I will call you – Peter – rock."

He also does that with us. He sees in us potential, ability beyond our sight, and invites us to embrace that potential in His power. It is His perspective, and He holds the power to unleash it. Our task is to simply yield to that power and let Him bring it to pass. That is certainly true in my life. I have discovered that God never leads us to do what we can in our own power but what we can in His. Thus He sees in us not what we are, but what we can be. Or maybe it is not what we see we are, but what we really are. I am the most unlikely to have success in any fashion as a pastor. In fact, as a young man, I sensed God leading me to become a pastor, and I knew this was not a good choice. I had an experience in a sixth grade speech class (I will share about that later) that proved any career with a requirement for public speaking was not an option for me. Pastoring, at least last time I had checked, required public speaking. God saw in me what I did not see, for that matter what others could not see. He knew that on my own I would never be able to speak publicly, but with Him I could do so with ease. He looks beyond that which others see to recognize that which is truly there.

Amazing, but without the right sight, you might consider an object trash when, in fact, it is a great treasure. Forget about what it was, and look at what it can be. Perhaps you have seen the little sign, "God Don't make junk", well he doesn't and you are certainly not junk. God has a specific plan for you and his plan will unleash a potential you may not even know you have. Ask God to give you insight into that plan, give yourself to it and you will become an example of a life transformed.

Chapter Seven

Worship With the Wrong Words

In a small, rural community, church – especially Baptist church – was predictable. Go to any small church in our county and the experience was pretty much the same, except of course, for the preacher. The churches in our area generally sang hymns out of one of three hymn books. Some churches used all three; they just provided additional information by telling the congregation, "take the red book, turn to hymn number 354, and let's sing the first, second and last verse." The standing joke of the day was that nothing was as lonely as the third verse in a Baptist hymnal. This was due, of course, to the fact that this verse was seldom sung.

Singing the familiar songs from the hymnal creates a unique challenge for those too young to read. We are forced to learn the words by memory – by listening. Needless to say, most children in the church knew what it meant to sing with confidence, loud confidence, on the song you knew or thought you did. One Baptist hymn offers a chorus: *"Bringing in the sheaves, bringing in the sheaves, we shall come rejoicing, bringing in the sheaves."* To young ears and minds, it is obvious, *"Bringing in the sheep, bringing in the sheep ..."* A song to be sung with gusto, I might add.

At Christmas we sang, *"Hark the hairy angels sing ..."* I never knew why we sang about hairy angels, but I did sing and with fervor. I knew I was especially talented because the older kids behind me loved my voice and often encouraged me to sing louder. Perhaps this was the early beginnings of karaoke? I am glad God says make a joyful noise and I am certain as I did, God laughed and accepted the song as from a pure heart of worship even with the wrong words.

There is a great lesson here. Worship is an active, participatory offering of our praise to a God worthy to receive it. I have heard it said that only Christians sing in their worship experiences. I am not sure if that is true, but we do sing. Singing seems to offer a natural outlet for the praise that builds within us as we reflect on our God. Often today we are tempted to attend church with an entertainment attitude. We arrive and sit waiting to be entertained or wowed by the musical abilities of those on stage. God has certainly given some a special gift musically and I do enjoy hearing them exercise that gift, but worship is not a spectator sport. One opportunity we all have to participate in a corporate worship experience is by singing. So next time you are at church – sing! Offer the words as an expression of your heartfelt praise for a God who deserves that and more. Be encouraged! You do not have to be good at it, in fact you don't even have to get the words right.

Chapter Eight

Attic Astronaut

O ne summer my dad purchased and installed a folding ladder to access the attic from the carport. Before that, there was a hatch type door that required a free standing ladder to access. Needless to say, the attic was not used for storage in those days. But when someone invented this neat folding ladder, attics across America were available to store Christmas decorations and junk previously assigned to a junk house out back. Maybe I need to explain, in the country, before self-storage units were available, people would often have small sheds or buildings behind their houses specifically for storage. Normally these houses were not organized, and generally contained a random collection of stuff too good to throw away, but requiring too much space to keep inside. Actually, they were the same as today's self-storage units, we just called them junk houses. Now back to the story, as a child, I was captivated by this ingenious contraption Dad had installed in the carport and would follow him into the attic every time this door was opened.

Growing up in a privileged time, I witnessed along with the world, as man took his first step on the Moon. America was full of great pride and optimism. I wanted to be part of it. As a result, playing astronaut was incorporated into my daily life. Now this thought may seem completely unrelated to our new attic stairs, but to me the correlation was easy.

One day Dad had been in the attic and left the ladder down and open. These rungs provided the perfect steps into the lunar module. Putting on my astronaut helmet (an old football helmet with the face mask cut off and spray painted silver). I entered the launch pad and with a final wave managed to pull the ladder up and close the door. Tucked away in the attic I began the necessary steps to countdown, hit zero, and blast off! I leaned back as the rocket began its ascent. My weight on the newly installed ladder was sufficient to throw the hatch open and allow me to fall backward and head first onto the concrete carport beneath. The impact knocked me out and broke the helmet, which saved my head. After an undetermined time I staggered to my feet, glad to be back on earth and ready to retire as an astronaut. My neck and shoulders were bruised for a few days, but after that all systems were go.

That experience taught me that, contrary to popular belief, just because a door opens before you does not mean you should walk through it. God does not always open doors before us, and not every door that opens before us is from Him. The key is to carefully calculate opportunities in light of the revelation the Father provides. This revelation is discovered through systematically reading God's word and continual prayer. You see, we are not taught to read the Bible to somehow make God happy or to please God with our dedication. We are taught to read God's word because it contains the words of life. It contains the insight we need to walk in the way He has prescribed. The disciplines of the faith such as prayer, meditation, reading, and studying the Bible are the essential steps that enable us to live as God directs. Just as an athlete or an astronaut lives a disciplined life to enable them to reach their goals; we must live a disciplined life to reach spiritual maturity.

Chapter Nine

It's About the Chickens, Stupid!

Grandma's chickens provided a lot of entertainment for us on Sunday afternoons. Often, Grandma would not gather eggs on Sunday morning so we could do the task on Sunday afternoon. After lunch one Sunday, I got the egg basket and headed to the hen house to collect eggs. The chicken nests were located in wooden boxes attached to the wall about three feet above the ground. There was a ladder that led to the boxes so the chickens could get to them. I was too short to see into the nest and too heavy to climb the small ladder so I would reach over the top or the nest to feel for the eggs and retrieve them.

I repeated this process several times, making my way down the wall reaching into each nest. As I reached into one nest, I felt a sharp pain like I had bumped my hand on a nail. When I looked at my finger, I noticed blood then looked back up at the nest to see a snake's head looking at me. I have been snake bit! I dropped the eggs and started toward the house. I started to run and then remembered, "No, the poison will go to your heart, walk slow, stay calm." With a gait equal to a half-walk and half-run, I made my way to the house, opened the door and announced, "I've been snake bit!"

"Where?"

"Here on my finger!"

"NO, where were you when you were bit? WHERE IS THE SNAKE?"

"In the nest!" "Grandpa, it's a chicken snake, go kill it!"

Everyone jumped up and went out to the chicken house! They left me standing there dying! As I was about to say, "Goodbye, cruel world," my brother said, "Stupid, chicken snakes aren't poisonous."

Often, right priorities are not easily recognized. The good really can become the enemy of the best. For my grandpa, finding and killing the chicken snake was the priority. My chief concern was tending to my life threatening injury. In the end, he understood the most important priority, and if they had given in to me, the snake might have escaped to return at a later time.

As a pastor, I see this all the time. In the church we do many wonderful things, but it is possible for the good things to get in the way of the main things. That is also true for our lives, isn't it? The good or the urgent can drown out the best. Perhaps one of the greatest tragedies in life is to spend all your life climbing the ladder of success only to discover in the end that it is leaning against the wrong wall. For that reason, it is imperative that we give ourselves to that which is important. The only way to make sure we have done that is to give ourselves what God says is important - to live by His standard. As the scripture says, allow Him to order our steps, or establish our direction (Psalms 119:133). A good start is to make sure you invest in the only thing that will last forever — people.

Chapter Ten

Fry, Fry Again

G randpa had a barn behind his house with a tin roof. The roof was accessible from the corral fence, and I would often cross the fence into the corral at that location. On a particularly hot summer day, my brother, our cousin and I were entering the corral when one of them said, "This tin roof is hot enough to fry an egg on." Fry an egg ... really? I know where I can get an egg.

I returned a moment later with an egg taken directly from beneath a hen. My cousin climbed on top of the barn, cracked the egg, and in amazement we watched as it sizzled, crackled and popped all the way down the roof to a semi-fried blob on the ground. "That was cool! Go get another!" Off I went to retrieve another egg to try again. Before it was over, we had fried at least a dozen eggs on the hot tin roof before we realized there might be consequences with these actions.

We quickly formed a loose knit pact, promising not to tell. All went well with our secret – even when Grandma expressed concern to Grandpa about the hens not laying eggs. Grandpa asked if we knew anything about that and, of course, we were clueless. About the time we thought all was forgotten, Grandpa asked us to go with him to the barn.

He led us to the back and pointed to a blob of fried eggs on the ground and some still hanging from the roof. I still remember that kicked-in-the-gut feeling and the disappointment in his eyes as he asked us why we did not tell the truth. I was the youngest, so it really wasn't my fault. No, that line didn't work with him either.

The scripture says, "Be sure, your sins will find you out" (Numbers 32:23). I have discovered that to be true, haven't you? Of course that verse must be taken in context, and Moses is referring to a specific sin with the nation of Israel. We know not all sin will be discovered in this life. It is possible to keep things a secret until we die, but there is One who does know. It helps when we live our lives with the awareness that God sees everything. We may get away with things because our parents don't know or our spouse does not know, but the truth remains that God does, and because He is a loving Father, He never lets us off. Living with awareness of His presence can keep us straight, but it can also keep us encouraged because the God that loves us too much to let us off also loves us too much to let us down, and too much to let us go.

Chapter 11

Do the Chicken Trance

Country boys have unique knowledge that is often unappreciated. For example, did you know it is possible to hypnotize chickens? Really, I am serious. My grandparents had chickens and when I acquired this valuable knowledge, I was somehow compelled to use it. Information of this nature is to be used so I determined to make application shortly after receiving it from a wise and trusted friend.

We would often eat Sunday lunch with my grandparents. Grandma had a picnic table with benches on each side. Fried chicken, fresh fried chicken, was a regular on the menu. When we finished eating, she would spread a tablecloth over the food and leave it on the table 'til supper. (Funny how I remember that, and even the color of the table cloth. Also funny that we would not think of doing that today because of food poisoning.)

Well, on one of those Sunday afternoons, I went to the chicken yard (pen) and performed hypnosis. Here is the secret: you catch a chicken, cup her wings in your hands, put her on the ground (it is best if you kneel on the ground behind), hold her beak to the ground and with your thumb or index finger draw a line in the dirt from the tip of her beak straight forward (in front) about six inches. Got it? Six-inch line on the ground, so she is staring at it, then just let go. She will stay with her beak on the ground staring at that line. Now, go get another chicken and repeat. We made designs with them, our initials ... oh, it is great fun! It works, trust me. Makes one wonder how this discovery was ever made.

As I reflect upon my childhood, I stand amazed at the wonder of God's creation. This story from my past reminds me of how our God ordered the universe, and in our world, gave man dominion over the animal kingdom. With dominion comes responsibility. It is not hard to find examples in our world of how man abused that dominion and the harm that followed. Animals, even chickens, have a place in the world's kingdom, but that place is in order under man. Some try to elevate animal life to a level equal to, or above that of man, and the result of that ideology is as damaging as the abuse of man's God-given dominion.

It is in that dominion that we can see a picture of God's unfailing love for us. When Satan first came to tempt Eve in the garden, he did so disguised as a serpent. I find that encouraging. God orchestrated, in that experience, an opportunity for escape. Remember, Paul says that in every situation God will provide a way of escape (1 Corinthians 10:12-13). I am convinced God would not allow Satan to come and tempt Eve as himself because she would not have been able to resist such a beautiful creature. But, when Satan came in the form of a serpent, he was coming in the form of a creature that God had already informed Adam and Eve that they had dominion over. They could have said no. Well, this is just a thought, or perhaps a reminder, that one can see God and the provision of God all around if he is willing to look.

By the way, the next week at lunch Grandma said, "I don't understand it, the chickens just quit laying eggs." Evidently, hypnosis does affect egg production – at least for a week. The next week things were back to normal.

Chapter Twelve

Busy as a Dead Chicken

My Grandma would often prepare fresh fried chicken. By fresh, I mean she would go to the chicken yard and select the chicken she was going to prepare while it was alive. Now, I realize that some of you believe the clean, packaged chicken bought from the grocery store arrived the way you bought it, and you have not entertained the idea that these were once live birds. But they were, and they were raised to provide food for your family.

I remember being educated about the process of preparing fried chicken by starting in the chicken yard. Actually, the chicken yard part was the most fascinating to me. I was never one to hang out in the kitchen. Grandma would select and catch the chicken and then with the flick of a wrist, "wring" the chicken's neck. She had done this so many times that one might say she had perfected the procedure to an art form. The process is considered a painless and humane way to kill a chicken, but I am not so sure. Have you ever witnessed this? The flick of the wrist breaks the chicken's neck, then the chicken is dropped to the ground where it now demonstrates a behavior uncharacteristic of something so close to death. The chicken begins to flop and flounce and run through the yard, wings flapping, but head in the dirt. The thing jerks and bounces sometimes several feet into the air, for at least four or five minutes. I must have stood wide-eyed and amazed the first time I saw this because I think Dad asked me if I was okay. This could be traumatizing for some kids. I think my response was, "Can I do that?"

Here is an interesting bit of barnyard wisdom. The chicken closest to death is the most active one in the yard. For a believer and a church, the application is a strong one. Activity is not necessarily a sign of life. Some of the most active churches have no real life; some of the most active believers have a heart that is far from the Father. It is not your calendar that determines the level of life – it is your heart. The temptation is to become so active that we literally do not have time for God, and the good does become the enemy of the best. Now, do not misunderstand me, activity is a good thing. James talks about the impossibility of us possessing a genuine faith that is not expressed in works and activity. (James 2:14-26) A real relationship with God, a growing, vibrant, thriving relationship is not measured in activity alone.

Enjoy the chicken.

Chapter Thirteen

"Hey Hot Shot"

O ne day I was visiting a friend who lived on a small farm. This farm was complete with the usual: chickens, pigs, cows and a large vegetable garden. The boy's dad was often buying and selling cattle and was involved in the normal transportation of the cattle that these transactions required. On this particular visit, my friend – who will remain nameless – introduced me to a new necessity in tending cattle.

Hot Shot — I should have paid more attention to the name than I did. A Hot Shot™ was a brand name for a type of cattle prod. It had a large, red handle filled with D cell batteries, attached to a long, slender fiberglass rod that had a red knob tip with two copper pins sticking out at the end. A button on the handle would deliver an electric charge to the copper pins sufficient to make a 2000 pound bull move.

He showed me how an electric arc could be seen between the pins when he depressed the button. We discovered it was even more impressive in a dark room. Our discussion eventually turned to how it might feel to get shot with a "hot shot." As with most conversations that went down this road, we finally agreed that we should find out. First he would zap me, and then I would zap him. Sounds simple, right?

It was at that point that I received a jolt from what would no doubt become the precursor to a police tazor. No words can truly capture the feeling of electrically charged pins against human flesh. The sound I made was sufficient to convince my friend that the deal was off! His only mistake was to drop the hot shot before he ran, well perhaps there was another. The length of the hot shot did not require that I run as fast as him to reach. One buzz to the middle of the back was enough to send him rolling head first in pain.

Now, when one has encountered such an electrifying experience, a desire is ignited within. A desire for everyone we know to have the same experience. To this day, a faint electronic buzz sound "moves me."

This device was created to help motivate cattle to move in a desired direction. I believe that, from time to time, we all need motivation to move. What is the "hot shot" that got you off to a fresh start? Identify it and use it. If you can't find one, let me offer a suggestion. How about living so that you can please our heavenly Father? How about the motivation of hearing Him say, "Well done you good and faithful servant"?

As you might be able to tell by this point in my writing, I had a great relationship with my father growing up. Often that relationship kept me on the "straight and narrow path." First, because I knew there would be consequences for my actions, but greater still the idea that I might disappoint my dad. You see, I had such respect for him that I did not ever want to disappoint or bring shame to his name. In the same way, when we have a great relationship with our God, we will be motivated to live in accordance with His desire for fear that we might bring shame or disappointment to Him. Proper motivation can get us going, and keep us on the right path.

If you are still struggling, I think a local feed store might offer a powerful solution. I think now they have a label that says these things are not to be used on humans ... ok, well I'm not sure it would have mattered.

Chapter Fourteen

Discontented, Technically Speaking

The speed with which technology has changed can make a young man feel old. For the first time in history, each generation will be able to remember inventions in their not-too-distant past that will be considered antique by the next.

My generation has been blessed to witness unprecedented change that has made us ancient in the eyes of today's teen. When I was a child, there were no personal computers, cell phones, dishwashers, ice makers, central air conditioners, GPS™, cable TV, microwave ovens, or DVDs. Perhaps the most amazing thing about this fact is that we managed somehow to survive.

I remember when dishwashers became available because I begged my dad to buy one. His response was, "Why buy one when I already have two?" referring to me and my brother. Yes, I was a dishwasher – and an icemaker. Ice in those days was made by pouring water into metal trays and placing them in the freezer. Oh, and I was also a TV tuner. We only had 4 channels, yes four, and the reception was from an antenna located on top of a pole behind our house. If we wanted to change channels, it was necessary for someone to go outside to turn the post to point the antenna in the proper direction for optimal reception. I also remember when an electric rotation device was invented for the antenna because I begged my dad for one, he said, "Why buy one when I already have two?"

This seemed to be his response for most new products designed to provide ease. Dad was never impressed with modern conveniences, and had no desire to "keep up with the Jones." As I look back on my life, I believe he possessed a gift that somehow enabled him to remain anchored to the things that matter. Perhaps it was connected to his childhood during the Great Depression. Whatever it was, the result was a simple and contented life.

Some of us chase every new gadget as if it will somehow make our life better. In the end, they never do. Just when you get that new gadget figured out and think others might be impressed, a new version comes out and the whole game starts over.

I think Dad was on to something. Stay focused on what is important, what matters, what lasts. The gadgets that are available are great and can offer comfort to our lives but only when they are not the focus of our lives. We can easily fall into the trap expressed by a not-so-popular song I remember which states, "Dear computer we adore thee, burdens are lifted by IBM." I am not sure who wrote it or who sang it, but I remember it and believe it reflects the ideology of our day.

Though I did not have access to the vast array of video games when I was a child, I still contend that some of the greatest games are the ones that require face to face interaction and imagination, the games and gadgets that focus on people and relationships. Technology has its place and does provide certain advantages, but it cannot bring happiness or contentment — those do not come with an electronic keypad.

Chapter Fifteen

An Unprofitable Profit

I n the small churches I attended as a child, parents would often give nickels, dimes or quarters to their children so they could give an offering during Sunday School. My parents were no different, and each Sunday I would head to Sunday School with my offering envelope to give to the Mission of the church.

Growing up as the son of the pastor of small rural churches meant that, for most of my life, I lived in the parsonage next door to the church. I soon discovered that children in possession of mission money in close proximity to my home were a winning combination. This observation revealed that I had an eye for business in my early childhood that I seemed to have lost later in life. That eye for business led me to step out as an entrepreneur and establish a small business empire.

Because I spent so much time outdoors, I became quite adept at finding and capturing animals. It was a skill that proved to be marketable. Each Sunday between Sunday School and "Church" time I would lead a group of children to my house where, for their mission money, I would show them the Animal of the Week. Baby armadillos were such a hit, I used them two weeks. Rabbits, raccoons, tadpoles, hornets' nests, turtles, snakes and even a formation in the creek bed behind my house that resembled a dinosaur track proved to be a virtual gold mine.

Then the popularity of the tour expanded into the adult market. My dad did not seem to appreciate my keen eye for business and shut down my operation while demanding I give restitution to our church's mission fund.

I told Dad in my defense, the Bible says, "In all labor there is profit, but mere talk leads only to poverty." (Proverbs 14:23) His reply? "Ill-gotten gains do not profit, but righteousness delivers from death. Proverbs 10:2" (Never use scripture as a defense with a pastor.)

I discovered that day that to take money committed to God and use it as profit is ill-gotten gains, but somewhere deep inside, I already knew that. Have you made the same discovery? Often pastors are ridiculed for any talk about money, but the Bible has a lot to say about our resources and how we use them. Perhaps a truth that gives us a glimpse of what the Bible teaches on the subject is from the words of Jesus when he says, "Where your treasure is there will your heart be also" (Matt. 6:21). These are truly powerful words. Words that offer us an opportunity to take a careful look at our life and determine what our priorities really are. Take a look at your business practices and the use of your resources. What does that look reveal about your heart?

Chapter Sixteen

A Moving Funeral

G rowing up in a pastor's home creates unique experiences and, in some cases, challenges. One such experience involves the exposure to death and funerals. Funerals were a normal part of our life since my dad was often called on to conduct them. Add to this fact that my mom was often asked to sing at the same service, and you are left with the understanding that I attended a lot of funerals. My older brother was generally charged with my care, and the charge was to sit quietly in the back until Mom could relieve him. Because we lived in a small community, most alternative babysitters were also in attendance at the funerals so I had to attend as well.

An event at my grandmother's funeral gave me a scare that actually followed me for several years and created a unique challenge for our normal method of handling funerals when all in the family were involved. When my family arrived at the funeral home for my grandmother's "wake," my aunt emerged from within, screamed and fainted on the front lawn. At the time I did not know what caused her distress, but I did know that anything that would cause that reaction was something I should avoid, so I refused to enter. I make light of it now, but it was quite traumatic for a seven-year-old child.

Shortly after this experience, I was once again required to attend the funeral of a man who had attended our church. Mother had to sing so I was naturally placed in the care of my older brother. My newly acquired fear of the dead almost created an impasse, but there was no other alternative available.

Now, the church where Dad pastored had just undergone some renovations to add air conditioning or a central air system as we called it. The building contained beautiful hardwood floors and was built just off the ground on piers. The contractor determined that the most efficient method of installing the A/C was to put the ductwork in the floors and, as a result, placed a large aluminum return air grill in the floor just in front of the center of the stage. Normally, a table occupied that spot and it was unnoticeable.

At this funeral, the casket was placed front and center, and the wheels of the cart supporting the casket were resting on that aluminum air grill.

For some reason the family had chosen to leave the casket open during this funeral. From my vantage point, at the side and front of the church near the piano, I could see the top portion of the... how can I say?... the dead man's face. Because of my earlier exposure to my aunt, I knew something bad could happen so I never took my eyes off the dead man. There is a strange but explainable phenomenon that happens when one stares at an inanimate object. Over time the inanimate object appears to move. As the service continued I noticed something that was extremely significant: this man was moving! At the exact moment of my critical discovery, two unrelated events happened simultaneously:

1. The brother of the older man who had died went into cardiac arrest in the service and made an awful sound. It was a deep, painful moan.
2. The weight of the casket broke through the aluminum air grill, and the entire casket dropped about 8 to 10 inches and tipped to one side! This time he did move.

And so did I! In a moment, a flash, I was gone. My brother, charged with my care, says that one moment I was there and the next I wasn't. Furthermore, had I not left a "water trail," he might not have known where to begin the search to find me.

It is ironic in some ways that I would end up as a pastor myself. God has removed my childhood fear of death. He did this by revealing to me that death did a terrible thing to Jesus, but Jesus did a wonderful thing to death.

He removed its sting. As I often say, because of Him death is not the end of the road, it is just a bend in the road – and He is waiting around the bend. Faith in Christ removes all concern of death.

By the way, there is an interesting story in the Old Testament about how the bones of Elisha caused a dead man to come back to life. I wonder how the pallbearers reacted on that day. You might want to check that story out, II Kings 13: 20-21.

Chapter Seventeen

Permission to Swim

In small country churches it is not unusual for folks to stand around after church services are over and just visit. This is true especially in the evening when it is cooler. Slowly, families leave until there are one or two families left, and they would often just move the conversation from outside the front door of the church to inside our house next door.

Generally, it was the same families that would hang out after church, and one of them had a son my age. I suppose that contributed to them often coming to our house because the boy and I would normally beat them there – which made it essential for the parents to drop by to retrieve their child.

One Sunday evening, several people were baptized during our worship time. At the end of the service, my friend and I went to the baptistery for a closer inspection. We had been there many times when it was empty.

Kids in small churches know that the baptistery is one of the best places to hide. On this evening, our interest was in the opposite direction. We decided that since it was full, there would be no reason for all that water to go to waste. What if we just took a dip? We talked about it for some time before reaching the conclusion that we should ask permission rather than seek forgiveness.

My dad was pastor, so he had the authority. Dad was visiting with several men when I approached with my request. It was one of those moments when he was not really aware of what I asked and he responded, "Go ask your mother." This was not unusual, in fact, it happened quite often. Though I did think it strange under these circumstances, I went to Mom. She was just as engaged with a conversation and responded, "If it is ok with Dad." Well, this is promising! Another trip to Dad saying, "Mom's ok if you are," yielded a simple nod of affirmation from Dad!

We couldn't believe it! Permission to swim in the baptistery! I was the first to do a cannonball and discovered a design flaw in baptistery architecture. Water displacement from a cannonball into a small, rectangular body of water within a church produces a tidal wave on the back row of the choir loft. We confined our play to more underwater activities after this discovery.

Later in the evening, my friend's family got ready to go home, and for the first time, we were missed. Their search finally brought them back to the church where, to their amazement – and mine – they discovered we were in the baptistery. Our dads immediately began to ask us what we were doing – no, what we thought we were doing and how we could ever dream this was okay.

"But you said we could!" I insisted. "We asked, and you said ask Mom. Mom said it's okay if you said it's okay. And you said it is okay so here we are!"

As a parent, I now understand what happened. Mom and Dad were not paying attention. I have done the same thing. Luckily, when I did, the results were not the same. I have discovered that life makes it difficult to pay attention. Distractions abound, each demanding our attention and action. Staying focused and tending to the issues of life are challenging. Not sure that ever gets easy, but I did learn that children are like a small fire. You'd better keep your eye on them or they can get out of hand and, if you are not careful, WITH your permission!

Chapter Eighteen

We Had a Blast After Church

Most of my childhood was spent in a church parsonage. Most of those parsonages (a home owned by the church and provided for the pastor) were next door to the church. The proximity of home to church was both good and bad. Every time we had church, I had friends over. Often the adults would stand around and visit so the kids could roam free until dark.

One Sunday night, one of my friends told me that if you shoved a potato up the tailpipe of a car, it would shoot out like a cannon when the motor started. Since I lived next door to the church and had access to potatoes, I felt that we should test this theory to see if this was true. I quickly retrieved several potatoes to make sure we had the correct size. We then surveyed the parking lot to select our victim. Once the car was selected, we shoved the potato into the tailpipe. My friend said it needed to be wedged in pretty good. We then found a place located a safe distance away to watch.

When the adults finally quit visiting, folks made their way to their cars. As the lady we selected attempted to start her engine, nothing happened. In fact, the car started but had no immediate response. About the time we felt like suckers, the car made a noise and the tailpipe produced a cannon-like explosion blasting pieces of potato through the parking lot. The lady was visibly shaken as she stopped and got out of her car. People were running up to her, and she was holding her heart – it was, well . . . great!

Until ... one of the men in the church picked up a piece of baked potato. He then cast an accusing eye in our direction. "Boys, do you know anything about this?" Well, of course, we knew a lot about this; we had masterfully tested the hypothesis of a theory and proved it right. This could be a science project. For some reason I sensed that the adults were not impressed with our research. Dad was not happy. He assured everyone he would take care of it, and he did! But, I do remember him trying to hide the smile when he told me Mrs. So-and-so almost had a heart attack. I love that about dads: they do know how to set us straight but deep inside they somehow respect, or appreciate the act. This fact must be concealed especially from moms who, by nature, do not always understand or value the behavior in question. Maybe girls do not have this thing inside them that just requires a theory be tested or a boundary challenged. My dad did see to it that I called the victim the next day to apologize. From then on, she always looked at her tailpipe before starting her car.

Two of my favorite descriptions of God are those which characterize Him as a good shepherd and those that present Him as a loving father. I saw the picture of God as a good shepherd years ago while visiting Israel. I remember the taxi of choice at the time was a Mercedes-Benz™ . That struck me as humorous. In America they were a luxury car, in Israel, a cab. On our free day in Jerusalem, my Tanya and I were at the sheep gate when a Mercedes-Benz™ cab pulls up. The back door opened and out climbs a shepherd and five or six sheep. That is right, sheep. I thought, "Wow! Now I get it, a shepherd in Israel loves his sheep enough that they haul them around in a Mercedes-Benz™ ." So when God says He is a shepherd, it is an expression of love and care. The other is the illustration of a loving father. Having a great relationship with my father allows me to relate to this concept of a loving father. In fact, the way my dad related to me on the occasion of the potato in the tailpipe allowed me to see and understand yet another great truth about our Heavenly Father. My dad did not back away from teaching me the wrong associated with my actions, but that faint smile let me know he understood what it was to be a boy, and the challenges that come with it. He handled me with love and grace as he taught me what is right and how to take responsibility for my actions. My Heavenly Father is like that. That is why He says, "Carroll, I am like a Father. I deal with you in love and with great understanding." This really became clear when I became a father. I remember when the nurse handed me my son and for the first time I held him. Something happened to me that I cannot to this day explain. But at that moment, that instant, all I had became his. My Heavenly Father loves me and you just like that. He never lets us off, but I know He smiles when He sees what we have done and as He leads us to handle it with His grace.

Chapter Nineteen

Six J's and an F

My best friend at one point in my life was Jeff. Jeff had six brothers and sisters so it was never dull at his house. The oldest daughter was Fern, and after her, the parents named each of the next six children with names beginning with a J: Joey, Jan, Jeff, Jerry, Jenny, and Joy. I can still hear their mom step out onto their back steps and call them to dinner ... "Joey, Jan, Jeff, Jerry, Jenny, Joy and ... Fern! Come to dinner!"

Someone has said there is nothing sweeter than the sound of your own name. I think that whoever said that was certainly not a guy given a name that is typically reserved for a girl. Growing up as a guy named Carroll in a rural setting was not easy. To make matters worse, there was a popular television show at the time called *Let's Make a Deal*. The host's name was Monty Hall, and his beautiful assistant was called Carol Merrill. Few days would go by in my early elementary years that someone did not call me Carol Merrill, forcing me to defend my honor.

When we moved next door to Jeff, I knew at our first meeting that introducing myself as Carroll would not be good. Now, for reasons I cannot explain – even as an adult – I hated my middle name just as much, in fact more, than Carroll. My middle name is Dean. I told you, I don't understand it. As I look back it would have been my name of choice, but not then — except when meeting a childhood friend equivalent to Huck Finn.

"My name is Jeff," he said.

"Mine is Dean." Before I knew what I said, it was done, and from that moment forward, I was Dean to his family.

I think it was my adventures with Jeff that gave me the grit to introduce myself as Carroll from then on. It still creates awkward moments, often for others more than me, but I'm okay with it.

Whether you like hearing your name or not, it is nice when others remember it. The Bible says that when we place our faith in Christ He writes our name in the Book of Life. One day, at the end of this life, we will stand before Him at that great roll call. On that day, I will rejoice to hear my name called and without reservation, I will respond.

Chapter Twenty

Shoes are for Sissies!

For some reason as a child, I had a strange aversion to shoes. There is something about running barefoot in the summertime that says Freedom, and I loved it! My love for this freedom always led to a time of negotiation with Mom as to when it was actually warm enough to be free of shoes for the summer. These negotiations were always connected to Mom's subjective notion of when it was warm enough to be barefoot without the risk of "catching cold." The battle typically began around Easter and lasted until she relented in late May.

With the announcement, I would run into the yard or to my friend Jeff's who, by that time, had already been free of shoes for at least two weeks. But, freedom always carries a cost. The cost in my case was stickers, thorns, rocks and hot asphalt. The first days of freedom always found me with bruised and bleeding feet. But, I knew the pain was always a necessary step in developing the hardened calluses that would allow me to run through the varied terrain of my outside world.

Some never know the sensation of cool grass on bare feet or the squish of mud surging between their toes. Some never venture out of their own comfort zone to know the simple freedom that awaits them. When the adventures of the new day are calling, you don't have time to put on socks and shoes! You must be ready to hit the ground running, unencumbered by such cares.

Perhaps you can draw your own application. Maybe this is a call for you to slow down and enjoy the simple things. Maybe it is a call to pay the price; push through the pain to embrace the benefit on the other side. I think I'll leave this one for you to figure out.

Chapter Twenty-One

Refrigerator Rapids

The creek behind our house provided hours of uninterrupted play time for Jeff and me. Our favorite place along the creek was a bluff that provided an almost straight drop - some twenty to thirty feet - to the shallow creek below. Ropes attached to a metal stake driven into the ground provided quick access to the creek below. When it rained it was not uncommon for this creek to swell out of its banks, but only once did I see it near the top of the bluff. It had rained for days, and much of the town was flooded. Rain put a damper on everything. My world revolved around outdoors and there were no video games, IPods, or computers when I was young.

After several days of being locked inside by the rain, a break in the wet weather brought an immediate response as Jeff and I headed to the bluff. On arriving, we were fascinated to discover the water near the top of the bluff and flowing with a power and speed we had never witnessed.

Jeff's older brother, Joey, had accompanied us to inspect the results of this flood. It was him who first recognized the possibilities before us and with unparalleled enthusiasm, demanded we follow him. We did. Off we ran to the back of the shop where Joey brought our attention to an old refrigerator his family had discarded some time earlier. "If we take the top off this, we can use it for a boat!"

This idea sounded like that of a genius, and we quickly began the rather difficult task of removing the door and motor from this Hot Point™ dinosaur. It took about four hours to dismantle and transport our boat to the bluff, and here we stared in wide-eyed excitement at the vast volume of water racing past in a torrent of foam, whirlpools and debris. We knew that to deposit our boat into this fast moving water would mean it was lost forever. So, we found a spot along the banks where we could secure the box against a tree, and to our amazement, the box needed no additional support from us since the force of the water kept it secure against the tree.

With boards that we had formed into crude paddles, we jumped in. It took all the strength we could muster to dislodge our craft from the tree, but in a moment we were free. In the next instant, we were being driven at high speed through trees and brush. Fear gripped us for a moment then gave way to the elation of a roller coaster ride. The paddles were of little effect in this current so we resigned to simply hang on. The fun turned to concern when we realized we had no plan to bring this ship to port. We were about to concede that we might be lost at sea before this was over. Then we noticed something ahead, a bridge - the bridge on Highway

6 going to town, at least six miles from where our journey began. The water was level with the bridge, and it was becoming clear we would hit the bridge. Logs in front of us hit it then disappeared beneath, emerging on the other side. This was not good. At the strategic moment our vessel turned sideways and hit the bridge. Joey yelled at that moment to grab the rail, and we did as our beloved vessel was sucked under the bridge never to be seen again. We struggled to the top of the railing and fell to the other side. With adrenaline pumping we began to yell, "That was great! Wow! Can you believe it?"

The six-mile walk back home was filled with the stories of this most excellent adventure. The event itself was never discussed in public; a pact made that day forbade its discussion until years later. A pact we all honored. For we knew the bluff might well have been banned forever if a hint of this found its way to the street. We were fortunate that Highway 6 was flooded, or there might have been witnesses.

Often we do not see the hand of God in our lives until we look back. He was there that day watching over three kids who had more guts than brains, and He has kept his hand on me since. A simple look back makes it evident. Even in the events that have tragic endings, a careful examination will reveal His hand at work. If there are angels assigned to watch us, mine is prematurely gray – like me.

Chapter Twenty-Two

Impossible? Not for God

I have always been aware of the fact: God has a great sense of humor. We see it in numerous scripture passages as Jesus speaks to His disciples and in the unique fashion that God has chosen to work in this world. I have also noticed this in the calling that He gives to all who are His. It seems to me that the qualification for serving God is a personal inadequacy. Not just feelings of inadequacy, but real inability. I am a testimony to this curious observation. I remember when I sensed God leading me toward a commitment to be a pastor. I was young when I sensed this desire or "calling," but I knew I was an unlikely candidate. Being a pastor involved public speaking, and my only experience with public communication had clearly been disastrous.

I was in the sixth-grade, in a small class, with a teacher who was a personal family friend. I say this to show it was a comfortable place. Eighteen close friends who I knew well – made a perfect audience for my first speech. I walked into class on my assigned day prepared and confident; but when the teacher invited me to give my speech, I froze. Fear gripped me like an iron claw. My heartbeat quickened and my eyes began to water. I remember thinking, "This is awful! My classmates will think I am crying." After a few moments of silence, the teacher offered a golden ray of sunshine. "Carroll, either come up here and give your speech or go to the principal's office." Without hesitation, I bolted for the door, making myself the promise that I would never speak in public.

Now God's plan for me involves something I cannot do. He has called me to the impossible, the unthinkable. When the thought of being a pastor first entered my mind, I immediately thought of my sixth grade experience. "You have got to be kidding," I thought. "Anything but that!"

Stories like mine seem to confirm the fears many have of God. The fear that He will call you to a life you do not want or that He will make demands of you that are impossible to accomplish. I have discovered, however, that you have no reason to fear God. He does ask of us that which we are incapable of doing, but only to demonstrate His ability to do it through us. His calling is an invitation to know His power, grace and mercy as we do the impossible.

Chapter Twenty-Three

Hot Pants

As a child, I loved holidays – especially those celebrated with fireworks. I would notice the local fireworks' stands set up along the highway and then begin to negotiate a ride to make a purchase. Fireworks in the simple times were more reasonably priced than today, and for a relatively small amount of money, one could secure hundreds of firecrackers and a good number of roman candles and bottle rockets.

As I mentioned, in the simple times of my childhood, little or much less attention was given to safety. Perhaps it was the experiences of my generation that provided sound evidence for a more intensive campaign for new safety programs.

After securing an ample arsenal of explosives, I would carefully and meticulously incorporate them into my play. I would often use them to blow up a model airplane as I played Army with toy soldiers, or I would light a firecracker and throw it as a grenade when I was the soldier. Either way, it made play time more fun and realistic.

No real concern for safety meant that we could throw firecrackers at each other, launch bottle rockets by hand – again at each other, and best of all, pelt one another with fireballs from a roman candle. I say that safety was not an issue then, but I know their labels clearly stated that these explosives were not to be held. But, as I recall, they did not say they were not to be fired at others, so the rule of personal safety was the only one we ignored, and we felt that this was personal risk to be taken at will by the person who purchased the fireworks. Oh, and by the way, there were no age requirements for the purchase of these products, or if there were we never knew it.

On one occasion, my friend Jeff and I ended up on opposing teams. I discovered he was a double agent, and my discovery of his identity led to a fierce battle. Armed with a pocket full of Black Cats and several roman candles, I eased around the house to position myself for a clear shot. When I got in position, I discovered Jeff had anticipated this maneuver and had launched a fireball that secured a direct hit. I did manage to turn in time to avoid a hit to the chest, but the turn allowed the fireball to land directly in my back pocket — the one loaded with Black Cats. This hit was a severe blow to my efforts since, in a moment, it ignited my weapon reserves. I am not sure how many Black Cats were in my pocket, but they all exploded. The back pocket was blown off, and I received significant powder burns on my bottom. I do not know the severity of the burns, and I was able to keep the jeans hidden until the wounds had healed. I do remember a rather large blister and the inconvenience it caused – especially when trying to keep it a secret.

The experience taught me that warning labels do serve a purpose. Somewhere at sometime someone most likely paid a price to discover something was dangerous. Often God's word provides us with examples of mistakes others make and the consequences of those mistakes. We would do well to learn from their experiences and not repeat those mistakes. Keep that in mind as you read scripture, and ask yourself these questions: "How can I avoid the mistakes others have made? Are there clear warnings God's word offers?" When you apply God's wisdom to your life, to your personal plans, you will avoid dangerous or painful events. Heed the warnings. Oh, and next time you celebrate a holiday with fireworks, don't keep the extras in your pocket.

Chapter Twenty-Four

Happy and Ringy

Dogs often get their names through some physical characteristic. At least that was the way it was in my house. We had several dogs during my childhood – each named because they "looked the part." We had a Pekinese named Barney because he looked like Barney Fife from *The Andy Griffith Show*. A beagle mix named Samson, "Sam" for short because he was unusually thick and strong across the shoulders; and then there was Happy because he was always happy.

Happy walked around with a smile on his face and a tail in constant motion. When you approached him, he would immediately roll over, hoping for a belly rub, even if a short one with your foot. He was a sweet dog, gentle and well ... happy. He was also a little rotund, or portly. I mentioned that I grew up in a simple time. Happy never tasted dog food. He simply ate our leftovers, or, as we called them – scraps. I might also tell you that he never went to the vet. Unheard of in our day, he ate all the stuff we know today would kill a dog – and he lived for 15 years. No vitamins or heartworm pills as I recall. He did get his annual shots, but by Dad who bought the serum from the local feed store. I could also tell you he was hit by a car on at least two occasions, bit by a snake once, and lived outside. Now that I think about it, Lucky might have been a more appropriate name ...

When we moved to the small town of Many, Louisiana, next door to Jeff, we naturally brought Happy. Jeff had a dog named Ringy who was white, except for a black ring around the base of his tail. From their introduction through a fence that separated our houses, it was hate at first sight. Any time anyone from our families went outside, Happy and Ringy ran to the fence, launched into a feverish snarling, growling, and teeth - showing fight through the fence.

The interesting thing about this behavior is that the fence that separated our houses was a single fence that stood unconnected to any other fence; in fact, the dogs could easily walk to the end of the fence and fight for real. On many occasions they would meet at the end, see each other growl, walk around in a circle, baring teeth, hair raised on their necks, and then run to opposite sides of the fence to duke it out. There were times when they would get into a real fight, but these were rare and would almost always end in their retreat to opposite sides of the fence to fight through the wire.

I have often thought about those days and those dog fights. Just as Happy and Ringy were enemies, we as the children of God have an enemy. He is relentless in his opposition and his pursuit of us. And the destruction he can bring is devastating. Yet there is an important truth we must never forget in this conflict. He is a defeated enemy. God has, in essence, placed a fence between us and him. Satan stands at the fence and is frightening but limited in power, and we are safe as long as we stay behind the fence. That is not to say that we cannot be hurt and that he cannot bite through the fence; he can. Even as a defeated enemy he can and does inflict damage, but that damage is temporal not eternal. He is there, and his growls and bare teeth can be frightening. But he is limited. We can stand against him in the power of the resurrection. Ringy was more agile and stronger than Happy, and really Happy was no match for him. Yet as long as he stood behind the fence all was well. It is the same for us. Stand firm in Christ, and He will stand between you and the enemy.

Chapter Twenty-Five

Three Longs and a Short

G rowing up in a day before cell phones required that parents be creative when getting in touch with their children. In the summer I would hit the ground early in an effort to pack as much life into the day as possible. Living in a rural area provided over 100 acres as our backyard. Our favorite place to play was a creek about one-half mile behind our house. Across a pasture and through a small grove of trees, you entered our version of Sherwood Forest. We spent hours there, sometimes returning just at dark.

No cell phones meant that during those hours of play, we were out of contact with our parents. They knew where we were or the general whereabouts within 50 acres or so. But, given a need, parental ingenuity developed a system to call us home. "Three longs and a short," meant three long blasts on the car horn followed by two short blasts, and you have an effective pager.

It was personalized, too; my buddy Jeff's call was two longs and a short. It seemed everybody in our part of the world knew the code, and on those rare occasions that we were playing near civilization, others might relay the message. "Son, your mother was calling you on the car phone, well, car horn."

I am amazed at how effective this form of communication was. We would play freely but with an ear toward home. Often one of us would say "Wait ... listen." At the suggestion each of us would freeze and listen for the horn. Without an attentive ear we would miss it, but we seldom did because the consequences were too great.

I have also discovered that to hear the voice of God I must live with an ear toward Heaven in awareness that at all times He might call. Often He speaks in a whisper, a still small voice as the scripture says (I Kings 19:12). The key is an attentive ear — one that will say, "Stop!" with such authority that our world stops as we strain to hear that familiar voice. For us, those three longs and a short come through reading, studying or meditating on His word. Read it with an attentive ear, the consequences of missing His voice are too great.

Chapter Twenty-Six

Orange Peel

A highlight for any week in the summer months was a trip to the grocery store with Mom. Piggly Wiggly was not an exciting store but in the same shopping center, next door in fact, was Gibson's department store. Gibson's was a small version of Wal-Mart or Target, in fact, local lore was that Sam Walton actually came and talked to the West Brothers - who owned Gibson's - to learn the business. (They must have been good teachers.)

Visiting Gibson's was like walking through a Sears *Wish Book*. (I'll speak to that later.) A boy could get lost in wonder without actually walking inside because every morning they would line their new bicycles in a row on the sidewalk in front of the store. While Mom was in the grocery store, Jeff and I (he always came along) could go next door to Gibson's. We would inspect each bike and decide which was the fastest and which we would buy if we had the money.

On one of those trips, the new model bikes had arrived. Smaller than the old bikes we rode, these new bikes had banana seats, sissy bars, reflectors, and high-rise handle bars. We stood in absolute awe and then, there it was! Unlike anything I had ever seen, "Orange Peel." That is right "Orange Peel" was the name printed on the side of this bright orange work of art. It had white hand grips on its high-rise handle bars, a white banana seat, and a stick shift. This bike had three gears with a stick shift! Jeff and I had never seen anything like it. It was amazing, life changing. Rarely does one have encounters of this nature in the course of a lifetime, in fact, some never do.

My life was now consumed with a fascination of "Orange Peel." We went to town every chance we could and spent as much time as possible admiring this ... engineering marvel. My only hope was that maybe ... Christmas. I knew it was a long shot but, "you have not because you ask not." So, I asked and I asked and I asked. In fact, I decided that this Christmas I wanted only one thing, "Orange Peel."

Summer turned to fall and fall to winter, but my resolve remained. At least until a trip to Gibson's in early December where, to my horror, I discovered that it was gone. I was crushed, but at the same time pleased that some kid in our town would come to school after the holiday to report that he (it was a boy's bike) was the proud owner of the coolest bike in town. I did not get upset - it was a long shot after all. So I quickly pulled out list number two. This one had more than one request. Orange Peel faded from my mind, filed away with all the other cool stuff I had encountered in my short life.

Christmas was exciting, but my new list did feel like a second choice. On Christmas day I got up early as was my custom, and entered the living room to see what the big guy had brought us this year. I froze. I couldn't believe it, there in front of my tree on Christmas morning was "Orange Peel," the coolest bike in the town. I owned the coolest, fastest bike in town. The responsibility was almost overwhelming. This was my best Christmas ever.

Could this be what God meant when he said, "You have not because you ask not?" I think so. I knew this was an impossible request and almost did not ask. I almost answered the request for my parents before I ever asked. I almost said no for them when they would have - and did say yes. How many times have you answered for God and chose not to bring your request to Him? How many times have we missed God's best because we simply did not ask? Of course God is not like a divine Santa Claus who sits in Heaven and fills our wish list. At times He will and does say no to our request, but He invites us to bring them just the same.

I've learned to ask for miracles and trust Him to provide. He has invited us to bring our requests - even the impossible ones. So I do, and many times I have discovered He is pleased to grant my request, and the impossible becomes reality.

Chapter Twenty-Seven

Wishing: By the Book

W hen I was a child, Christmas officially began when the Sears
catalogue *"Wishbook"* came in the mail. Two other stores had
Christmas catalogues – J.C. Penney and Montgomery Ward, but neither
rose to the level of the Sears catalogue. When you lived in the country,
before WalMart came along, your best option for Christmas shopping
was through the mail. I am not sure when the catalogue arrived each
year, but its arrival marked the beginning of the holiday season.

My brother and I would fight over the catalogue, and we logged hours
looking at it. The *Wishbook* was the apex of marketing, and each toy was
set against a backdrop so spectacular that the toy itself was elevated to
a level it could never truly live up to. It was in this book that the final
decisions would be made, and the final list completed before we mailed
it off to Santa.

In rural America there was no mall so Santa was not readily available. Oh, he did make appearances from time to time, but the cotton beard that was loosely attached to an elastic band coming from under his hat was suspect. If that was not enough, the black, plastic leggings pulled over the top of black dress shoes, designed to give the appearance of boots, was an insult to even the most hopeful of small boys. No, the best bet was to send the big guy a list and not trifle with these wanna be's. But for me, it all began, not with Black Friday or Cyber Monday, but with the *Wishbook*. It was that random day when the *Wishbook* arrived unannounced that summoned us into the world of Christmas.

Honestly, I regret that children no longer have that experience. Oh, it's better today; there are fewer hokey costumes, and some Santas make big bucks impersonating the ole guy. I hear they even have a union. No, our children get the best today – interactive websites have replaced the *Wishbook* along with the need for an active imagination to bring the toys alive. It is better now – more predictable and trendy Christmas décor is in the stores in October. It is better now – Christmas shows are on DVD's to be watched any time. In my day, the annual television viewing of *Rudolph the Red-Nosed Reindeer,* narrated by Burl Ives, required planning, lest you miss until next year. No, it is better now – now that the *Wishbook* is online ... or is it really better?

Could it be that all the things that make Christmas better have allowed it to get lost in the mix? Maybe it wasn't the *Wishbook* that made Christmas special – it was Christmas that made Christmas special. In simpler times, it was just easier to enjoy. Easier to focus — easier to relax – easier to be simple.

I have often heard an ole adage that can help govern the basic management of business ... K.I.S.S. Keep It Simple Somehow. Good advice, especially for the holidays. For me, a more pointed interpretation offers a more pointed admonition. Keep It Simple *Stupid*. This year, make the K.I.S.S. principle a part of your Christmas celebration.

Chapter Twenty-Eight

Mr. Pouncy

Today elementary, middle, and high schools have police officers assigned for security and order. In our elementary, we had a Mr. Pouncy. Believe me; he was more frightening to a grade schooler than any policeman. Mr. Pouncy was our principal. I am sure he was a gentle and kind man. I am certain that he loved children and was probably a good administrator. To a grade school boy, his tall, slender build and stern demeanor was ominous. There were stories about him and his paddle - stories of other children who had misbehaved, been sent to his office and never seen again. I am not sure about the stories of students who were sent to his office and never seen again, but I can attest to the fury of his paddle.

My first encounter with this legendary man is seared into my consciousness. I was sent to stand in the hall by my teacher. I am not sure what happened, though I am somewhat certain of my innocence. Whatever the offense, it was big enough that the teacher felt I should leave the room, but not bad enough to be sent to "the office." Mr. Pouncy was known to walk the halls looking for those who had been excused to the hall.

Shortly after being sent to the hall, a large, tall figure appeared at the other end of the hallway. I began to become as small as possible and pray that God would be merciful. Mr. Pouncy emerged from the shadows and, in his best James Earl Jones voice, asked why I was in the hall. My response was, "She," pointing to the class, "sent me here." "Meet me in my office," was his reply. I went to his office and waited with three other boys in one of five straight-back chairs against the wall. On the floor in front of us were two black lines, each about six feet long running parallel to one another. When he arrived, he spoke without so much as a glance in our direction, "This line," pointing to the one closest to him, "is the going home line. This," pointing to the other, "is the paddling line. Get in one of them."

All three of us slowly stood and moved to the paddling line. Legend or not, I knew if I went home, it would be worse there than here. One by one, Mr. Pouncy applied the board of education to us and sent us back to our classroom.

I am certain that the no-nonsense approach of this principal and the support of parents who understood the value of discipline, allowed the police to stay on the streets. We did not need them at school, we had a Mr. Pouncy.

Times were different then. Parents were more willing to discipline their children and allow their children to be disciplined. Adults were in control and made decisions, not children. Parents seemed to know that children needed correction. When did that change? No really, when did that change? I am not sure but it is evident it has; children are in control now, and children make the decisions for the family. Children decide where the family will eat and what they will do for entertainment; for the most part they rule in many families.

With this shift, it is easy to see why we are in trouble. Children are not equipped to make decisions and should not be in control. I heard a great quote a few weeks back that puts this issue in perspective. Coach McCoy, the father of Colt McCoy who now plays for the Cleveland Browns, was speaking about a decision he and his wife made with regard to the rearing of their sons. He said, "We determined to prepare our sons for the path not the path for our sons." Now that is huge so think about it for a moment. Preparing our children for the path means to instill within them character traits so they are prepared to handle the situations of life. Preparing the path means parents get involved to make sure that all is well and our children never face tough times or situations that challenge. Preparing the path means the parents intervene to ensure that their child never experiences anything one might see as negative. To prepare the child means discipline is a must while to prepare the path means we protect them from anything harsh, which many mistakenly interrupt as discipline. Well, my folks and most parents of my generation were committed to prepare the child for the path not the path for the child. That is the right choice, and that was certainly the aim of Mr. Pouncy.

Chapter Twenty-Nine

Peach Tree Discipline

T he book of Proverbs in the Bible speaks frequently about the value of discipline. For some reason, I believe my dad was particularly fond of those passages. He certainly – in my mind – was committed to living them out. Proverbs 12:1 states, "Whoever loves discipline loves knowledge, but he who hates reproof is stupid." As a child, I was, well ... stupid, 'cause I hated discipline. I never learned to like it until I left home and, looking back, recognized its value in shaping my life.

I am sure my dad and mom struggled in the discipline department -all parents do. But, if they did, I never noticed. In fact, it sometimes appeared that my dad enjoyed it. Oh, he was not abusive, but he was quick to offer reproof and even give other adults permission to exert whatever force might be called for to bring me in line.

Now, Dad was old school and had no place for discipline techniques like "a time out" or "stand in a corner." His belief was that a quick, decisive blow to the backside could change behavior and attitudes. Dad's weapon, I mean devise of choice, was a belt. I think because it was always near (see quick and decisive above). He could remove his belt in one motion and apply it to my backside in a second with profound accuracy.

On one occasion, I entered into a conversation with a friend about this discipline thing and discovered that his dad did not use a belt; he used a switch. My knowledge of the pain inflicted by a belt led me to think my friend had a better deal, so the next time I got into trouble, I stopped Dad – belt in hand – and demanded he use a switch instead. I still remember his bewildered look. "You want what?" " I want a switch!" "Okay," he said. "Go get one."

For any of you who have knowledge of switches, you will appreciate my selection. I went out back and cut a long, keen branch from a peach tree. Yes, a peach tree. For those of you who are not familiar, no words are adequate. The pain that a peach switch can impart to the bare legs when applied by a master of the craft of spanking is unbearable. I believe untold information could be acquired from terrorists if our government would apply a peach tree switch to their hind parts.

I never asked for a switch again and, when I told my friend about it, his response was the same as my dad, "You did what?"

I think that peach tree switch led me to dislike discipline. Maybe one reason is that no one appreciates the discipline when it is applied, and no one likes to apply it. We all understand its profound value and the dangerous result of its absence. Often, our appreciation does not come until after the fact. Perhaps that is why the writer of Proverbs speaks so often about discipline. He knew as parents we would need encouragement to stay strong in our commitment to apply it, and as individuals we would need to be reminded of its value in our lives.

Chapter Thirty

Stinkin' Up the Night

M y dad would often offer words of wisdom or quotable quips when he taught. This practice carried over to his parenting as well. I remember him saying, "Son, a bulldog can whip a skunk every time, but is it worth it?" That one has served me well in life. Think about it. Another that seems to touch on the same meaning was, "You can win the battle and lose the war." These old sayings or quips are easy to remember and seem to provide a vivid picture of the truth they set forth.

The power of the skunk saying came home when I was around 13 years old. I would often go coon hunting late at night with light, gun and dog. I could walk directly behind our house and be in the woods hunting in a matter of five minutes. A friend had come for a visit, and we decided to make a quick hunt. All went well and after a couple of hours, we began to make our way home. Through the woods and past the pond, now just across the pasture, I could see the lights of home. We were walking single file in a cow trail when suddenly Gary threw his light into the air and yelled, "Run!!" Startled by the sudden yell and the flashlight swirling through the dark, I didn't ... run.

As I turned my light toward the ground in front of me, I saw a skunk hopping backward with its tail in the ready position. I turned to run but the skunk's reflexes were quicker than mine, and he got me. I cannot describe the level of disgusting, awful, sick yuck I immediately experienced. My nose burned, eyes watered, stomach churned. A skunk's defense is as powerful as the bite of a cobra. I spit, sputtered, threw up, coughed, and the intensity seemed to grow.

As I arrived at the back door, I was met by the merciful, sensitive, caring voice of my dad who said, "Don't you come in this house!" I spent that night outside. In fact, I think I spent several nights outside. And in case you are wondering, nothing works. Nothing. As news spread, solutions for my dilemma began to pour in. I tried them all, and none worked. Tomato juice bath doesn't work. Ketchup, no. Alcohol, might as well drink it. This stuff has to wear off. I think the only thing the suggested remedies did was to add a new fragrance to the mix.

That encounter has had a lasting effect. To this day, I get nauseous when I smell a skunk. The old saying my dad offered was intended to teach the importance of wise choices. Just because you can do something doesn't mean you should. But for me the real lesson was the importance of making the wise choice to heed the warning of a faithful friend. When someone you trust says run, you run and ask why later. I am grateful that God has placed faithful friends in my life who often offer sound advice and wise counsel. Friends sometimes stand at a different vantage point and can see things we cannot. I have a tendency to challenge their counsel and sometimes become frustrated if they do not see things like I do or endorse my plan. Yet, again and again I have discovered the wise perspective of a trusted friend is a valuable resource. Perhaps the key here is "trusted" friend. If the friend who offers the advice is a trusted friend, it is worth a break to consider the counsel. The scripture says, "Faithful are the wounds of a friend" (Proverbs 27:6). It is a good thing to have a friend that will be honest even when it hurts. It is also a gift to have a friend who will warn you of impending danger, but it is up to you to heed that counsel. If I had listened to my friend, I might have avoided a miserable experience.

Chapter Thirty-One

Some Secrets Aren't for Keeping

Living in the country required some creativity in play. We had no Playstation™ or Nintendo™, and cartoons only aired on Saturday morning. But, give a kid a BB gun, and he will find ways to entertain himself.

One summer day, my friend David called to tell me a man had come to bush hog (a mower behind a tractor) the pasture behind his house. Bush hog + high grass + a good BB gun = a rat killing! Rats like the tall grass, and as the mower makes its way around the field, there are fewer and fewer places to hide. The result? Well, the rats make a brave dash for the woods, and we are waiting. Sounds like fun, doesn't it?

David also had a dog that would accompany us on these ventures, and he would often alert us to the prey. On this particular day, we noticed the dog digging frantically. Convinced he was unearthing some kind of varmint, we stood ready. After a moment of digging, a small hole appeared and a bee emerged, landing on the dog's ear. He was then joined by another who settled on the dog – stinging his nose. David and I just stood there amazed. No rats, just bees. Bees! In an instant we were covered in bees, and as we ran, they followed. They invaded my shirt, so I threw it off. In my pants, they can have them too. When we arrived at the back door, we had provided the neighbors a show, a' la Chippendales.

The bees won; a BB gun is no match for hundreds of mad bees. I don't remember how many stings we received, a bunch. I do know, however, that if you get bees in your britches, others will know about it.

I have often thought about that day. There are some things that happen to us that should be obvious. As a Christian, our relationship with Christ is one of them. Our relationship with Christ should impact every part of our lives. Knowing Him is like having bees in your britches – everyone should know it.

Chapter Thirty-Two

Let the Dead Bury the Dead

O ne of the churches my dad pastored had a graveyard in the back. Actually, it was behind the parsonage where we lived. The woods I normally played in were just beyond the cemetery so I would walk through on my way to my summer fun. The land on which the church and cemetery was built was hard, red clay. This clay created a challenge for grave diggers because of its sticky texture.

One day a member of our church died and was buried in that cemetery. The night following the funeral, we experienced a hard, flash flood type rain storm. The rain and its runoff quickly settled to the bottom of the freshly dug grave. The clay would not allow for quick absorption. So, the grave filled with water and floated the casket to the top. The downpour of rain washed the dirt off the top so that by morning, as the water drained into the ground, the casket settled to the bottom with no dirt on top.

The morning after this rain, I got up to head to the woods and as I walked through the cemetery, I stumbled upon an open grave with a casket in the bottom. Dad was not home at the time, so I convinced my mom to come observe my discovery. Reluctantly she went with me, and just as I had reported, there was the open grave. She quickly determined what happened and told me I would need to bury him. Armed with a shovel, I tackled the wet, sticky clay and after a few hours had managed to fill the grave.

That next night, another thunderstorm created the same scenario and a new discovery the next morning. In fact, it rained every night that week, and I buried that guy at least four times. By the fourth time, I was putting bricks and rocks in the hole and even begged Dad to park the car on the grave to keep this guy from coming to the surface. I told my dad after the fourth time that perhaps the country song popular at the time was true, "You Can't Keep a Good Man Down." I also told him that Jesus said, "Let the dead bury the dead," and if he comes up tomorrow some of the other residents of the cemetery could pitch in.

Some things refuse to stay buried, have you noticed? We try to push it down, and then a storm comes and they are once again exposed. Anger, jealousy, and bitterness, are just a few we often work hard to repress. At times we are convinced that we have conquered the beasts until an unexpected storm hits, and from the depths of our heart they emerge. Maybe the problem is that we bury or repress these rather than dealing with them. It is easier and less messy to push them aside and pretend all is well, but they will be back. I have discovered that God in the person of the Holy Spirit can enable us to deal with the issues of life. He gives us the grace for the disappointments of life and strength for the struggles of life and hope for the future. With God's help, we can deal with the issues that continue to surface and put them to rest once and for all.

Chapter Thirty-Three

IF DOGS COULD TALK ...

David had a dog named Snoopy. Snoopy was an inside dog, and that was cool because we had an outside dog. I always enjoyed playing with Snoopy when I went to spend the night at David's. One night as we got ready for bed, David let Snoopy out in the backyard. After a few moments he opened the sliding glass doors and called for the dog to come in. Several calls, but Snoopy was not interested so David closed the door.

A moment later, Snoopy decided to return and ran from the back of the yard to what he thought was an open door. He hit the glass door with a bang, and when we arrived to see what had happened, Snoopy was staggering across the yard. Through the laughter we tried to console him and then wondered if he would do it again. We waited a while then let him out. He wandered in the yard then we called energetically and eased the door shut. Snoopy came full speed and slammed into the door. Now, I know you are thinking, "How mean!"

Hey, all we did was call him – he ran into the door. Good news? He did not fall for that trick again. We tried. He learned from his mistake. My dad used to say often, "Son, you don't learn from what you do right, you learn from what you do wrong ... but learn!" What is the ole saying? "Fool me once shame on you, fool me twice shame on me?" I think that is it. Learning from our mistakes is vital to our survival. Perhaps that is one reason why God wants us to confess our sins. To confess means to agree with. God says if we confess our sin He is faithful and just to forgive us and cleanse us from all unrighteousness (1 John 1:9). God certainly forgives but His forgiveness does require our agreement that it is sin. That is our confession. Another part of the process is an often neglected component, repentance. Repentance means to turn from my sin to God. That does not mean that we will never commit the same sin again because we will, but the process of repentance and confession brings an awareness and dependence on God that will teach us.

Chapter Thirty-Four

Go-Cart + Chain Saw = Fantastic!

B y the time I was in seventh grade, I had worked enough jobs that I had amassed a sizable war chest. When you live in rural USA in the simple times, work opportunities abound, even for young boys. Farmers in our church always had an odd job for any boy willing to work hard, and I always availed myself of those opportunities.

My dad did a reasonable job teaching me how to handle money – though I seemed to follow his advice more carefully as a child. His encouragement to save meant that when rare financial opportunities became available, I could move. Like a used go-cart frame in excellent condition for $30 and a well-used chain saw for a bargain, $15. For $45 and a lot of mechanic work, I had an investment opportunity that comes once in a lifetime. I was able to scavenge enough parts from other chain saws, donated to my cause, to put the motor in good working order. With some impressive engineering, I was able to mount the motor on the frame and add a centripetal clutch, and I was in business!

The maiden voyage revealed immediately that some critical issues were not quite resolved. The location of the kill switch would need to be moved since I could not safely – and I do emphasize SAFELY – reach it from the driver's seat. The motor was located directly behind the driver seat so getting up on ones knees to reach the kill switch behind meant divided attention between where I was going and where I had been. This was not conducive to keeping your eyes on the road. The throttle cable would need to be adjusted also so that it would not stick in the "Full" position. Moving at top speed was fun but there is an advantage to slowing down when you release pressure on the gas pedal. The maiden voyage was fun for a moment, and then fear gripped me and held me until at last I was able to get on my knees in the seat and reach back to trip the kill switch, and then it was FANTASTIC!

Amazing how our perspectives change. Often the most frightening times in our lives can become the most fantastic. You may - in fact you will - at times feel that life is racing out of control. Fear will grip your soul. But God has promised that He will never leave us or forsake us. I love that verse in Hebrews 13:5, "I will never leave you or forsake you." In fact in the original language the verse contains a series of double negatives. To translate literally would be poor English, but it is great theology. This is a literal translation; "I will never, no not ever, no never, leave you or forsake you." Now that is encouragement, when life is full speed and out of control, He is there. Another promise from Romans 8:28 tells us that this same God will use every situation we face, even the bad ones, for our good and His glory. He will take the bad experiences of our lives and use them for our good. Wow.

So, hang on and enjoy the ride! By the way, we clocked my go-cart at 55 mph. Not bad for $45 and I sold it for more. Fantastic.

Chapter Thirty-Five

Get Off the Fence!

One of our neighbors had several head of cattle in a pasture behind his house. At some point, he must have had trouble with his cows getting out or stressing his fence lines as they pursued greener grass on the other side. Whatever the reason, he had found an effective solution by placing a single strand of electric fence wire along the top of his existing fence. An electric fence is designed to emit a current that, when touched, will deliver a shock packed with just enough power to make one wish he had not touched it AND enough to convince you not to touch it again.

His solution to his livestock issue would not have been my concern, except that his property provided a short cut between my house and David's. One evening I was at David's, and we decided to take the short cut to my house. We were aware of the electric fence and would often walk the perimeter of the pasture rather than the straight shot across. On this day, however, we were in a hurry and decided to take the true short cut through the field.

Now, the charge on an electric fence is normally intermittent, meaning it can be set to deliver a charge for a prescribed number of seconds then stop for another prescribed number of seconds. As we approached the fence, I turned my hand, palm toward the top "hot" wire and rapidly touched the wire to see if it was on. My hesitance to touch the wire led me to move quickly toward the wire, getting closer and closer until I had actually touched it.

My timing must have been in sync with the wire's prescribed timing because, as I made contact with the wire, there was no shock. Realizing this, I let my hand settle onto the wire and confirmed that it was off – at least for that moment. I told David the fence was off and grasped a post and began my ascent. As I put my left foot on the second wire and swung my right over the fence, my inner thigh came in contact with the electric fence that had now arrived at the prescribed second for ignition. The inner thigh is a highly sensitive area of the body and, when in contact with an electric current, causes an involuntary jerk away from the source of pain. The problem with this reaction is that the movement in one direction simply applied contact with the other inner thigh. I bounced back and forth until I fell and hung upside down from the fence.

David tried to help but when he touched me, the shock went through me to him and his involuntary reaction was to let go, allowing the pain to return to my legs. I finally came free from the fence and fell to the ground, exhausted from the ordeal.

The moral of the story is to be careful of short cuts. Taking the fast, easy way out of a situation often leads to a result you may not desire. But even with this admonition, we are always looking for the easy way out, a short cut. I remember my dad once told me, "When God wants to build a strong oak tree, He takes years, but when He builds a squash, He takes a few weeks." Others have considered this human tendency, and ole sayings abound to characterize the truth. No Pain, No Gain, for example. It seems in this high-tech generation we are even more committed to finding an easy way to do everything and the short cut has become the norm. In our walk with God, there are no short cuts.

There are no Cliff Notes™ or *Reader's Digest* version of scripture that will produce maturity. Perhaps that is why today, as in Paul's day, we have people who have walked with God or have known Him long enough that they should be teaching and mentoring others but instead continue to be in need of teaching themselves. They still need a steady diet of milk when by now they should have moved on to the meat. A pastor friend in Baton Rouge used to say it is sweet to see a baby drink milk from a bottle, but there is something disgusting about a guy who must part his whiskers to get the bottle into his mouth. For many believers, years of going to church has not deepened their relationship with the Lord because church attendance has become a substitute for personal time with God and personal study. To grow in the Lord, we need time, effort, and energy. There truly is no short cut to spiritual maturity, and the

Christian life is not for sissies. Maybe it is time to take a quick assessment of your spiritual life and progress. Maybe it is time to step up and make the commitment necessary to grow in your relationship with God. The alternative could be shocking.

Chapter Thirty-Six

A Party Line

When I was in the seventh grade, our telephone was on a party line. Now, I must immediately explain for those of you that were not so privileged: a party line, often common in more rural areas, meant that we shared our phone line with four other families. Well, actually eight, but that would take even more time to explain.

Sharing a phone line meant that the phone in our house was like an extension in someone else's. If I was using the phone and you were on our party line, you could pick up your phone and hear my conversation. Now, you might ask this question: "When the phone rings, does it ring in every house and if so, how did I know if it was for me?" Well, the answer is yes. If you call me, the phone rang in every house on the party line, but the ring was unique. The phone company assigned specific ring patterns to each number. If someone was calling us, the phone would sound three long rings and one short buzz. I'm serious. If it were someone else on the party line, it rang their pattern, one long and three shorts or two longs and a short.

Needless to say, when the phone rang - even in the middle of the night you listened for your pattern. Often you would hear the phone ring, and Mom or Dad would yell, "Is it for us?" Oh, they yelled because we only had one phone, which was on the wall in the kitchen. And no, it did not have an earpiece you held to your ear while talking into the wooden box!

If you accidentally answered the wrong ring, phone etiquette required that the right person yell at you for listening in on their call. (Not really but that is what happened.) I still remember the sound of three longs and a short. We have come a long way from party lines to cell phones. From a simple, assigned ring pattern to a myriad of choices in ringtones, but we must still keep our ear attuned to the ring.

As a child of God, we have been provided with a private line. As a part of having a relationship with God, we have access to Him at any time. We have the ability to talk with the creator of the universe and call Him Father. This privilege is ours through faith in Jesus Christ, for it is through Him and His work on the cross that this access is available. It is in that access that we find the strength, wisdom and grace needed for daily living. Jesus taught us the value of this opportunity by example. He spent his entire ministry going from one place of prayer to another, and it was in between those places of prayer that he ministered to others. This was such a visible and vital part of His life that the disciples asked Him to teach them to pray. It is interesting that they never asked Him to teach them anything else. In response He gave them what we often call the Lord's Prayer (Matt. 6: 9-13). I believe this prayer gives us a pattern to follow in our prayer time. Though I am tempted to walk you through it, I might instead just suggest that you spend some time praying. Do that and you will find that prayer is the greatest power we have available to us since it connects us to His heart. Prayer is a two-way street: we talk to God and He talks to us. Make time for it and keep your ears open and your heart attuned to His call.

Chapter Thirty-Seven

Thirteen Snakes

I t might not surprise you to discover that, as a child, I liked snakes. I would look at pictures of snakes in the encyclopedia and would even check out books from the library on the subject. That demonstrated "interest" since I never checked out or read any books - other than the encyclopedia. I was careful to learn the difference between venomous and non-venomous snakes and embraced the philosophy that non-venomous snakes were our friends and the only good venomous snake was a dead one. That philosophy does not make me a snake lover, but I do have a fascination with the harmless sort.

My fascination would result in my own version of a capture and release program. I would capture, play with, and release snakes on a regular and consistent basis. At some point, I acquired an old aquarium which allowed me to keep my prize for a longer period of time. Case in point, a garter snake named Gertrude. I was especially fond of her and kept her for several weeks. During that time, I witnessed a unique phenomenon in the reptile world. Garter snakes are the only species of snake that give "live birth," and Gertrude allowed me to learn that lesson firsthand. In the fullness of time, she gave birth to thirteen babies right there in my aquarium.

I learned another lesson that day. Not everyone is happy or amazed by the spectacular and miraculous arrival of thirteen baby snakes; my mom was one of those people.

As a result, my joy was met with an insensitive demand that I release Gertrude and her children. I was able to avoid an immediate release by informing Mom that the babies were too young but that I would release them in a day or two. She reluctantly agreed but reminded me almost hourly that I might need to be more concerned for my own survival because if these snakes got out in the house, my life was over.

The next evening we returned home from church, entered the back door, and turned on the kitchen light just in time to see a baby snake slither across the floor. Mom quickly retreated to the garage and demanded to see and count thirteen snakes brought to her and released away from the house. I quickly caught the babies and one by one brought them past Mom. One, two, three ... ten ... and then – nothing. I searched everywhere, but no more snakes. My explanation was rejected, and Mom refused to enter until all thirteen snakes were accounted for. After an hour of searching, I was still empty handed. At that point, Dad suggested I show Mom the same snake three times or we would never get her in the house. I did, and with secure satisfaction she returned home. Fortunately, the final three were never seen again and Mom never knew.

Proverbs 13:1 says, "A wise son heeds his father's instruction, but a scoffer does not listen to rebuke." Had I listened to my mom and released the newborn snakes, I could have avoided the rebuke. But, because I listened to my father, my life was spared.

Chapter Thirty-Eight

Don't Swallow Your Sin

My upbringing seemed to echo the humorous observation of a comedian named Grady Nutt. Before his death, I was blessed to have heard him perform live and in person. He claimed that he, "grew up five miles from any known sin." He also said, "There were three rules in his church: You won't smoke, you won't drink and you won't want to."

My dad had similar rules and, like Grady, I had a problem with wanting to. Living in the country meant you could be employed at a young age. Once you were big enough – not old enough - to drive a tractor, you had a job. I can't remember how old I was when I was big enough, but it must have been 12 or 13. My first job was to drive the farm truck and haul seed to the guys planting soybeans. Eventually, I earned a spot driving the tractor.

One morning one of the guys I was working with offered me a chew of tobacco. "It will help keep the dust out of your throat," he said. Hmmm, tobacco. The rules never said "no chewing" so I said, "Sure." He forgot to tell me to spit! I know, he thought I knew, but I lived five miles from any known sin. No one had ever shown me how. My granddad dipped snuff and he had a spit can, but I never put the two together, okay? Besides this was not snuff, it was plug tobacco, "Ole Mule" … no "Brown Mule."

I popped the plug in my mouth and chewed it like bubble gum. He said it was a chew. The stuff produced a lot of juice, thus keeping the dust out of my throat. I chewed and swallowed and all was well for about five minutes. Then I began to feel strange. The front wheels of the tractor seemed to be moving in and out and suddenly from deep within, my stomach rejected the tobacco juice and sent it back up with everything else that was in there. I do not recall ever being as sick, unless it was the time Dad caught me smoking and made me smoke a huge cigar as quickly as possible.

I suppose the real lesson for me was to be careful what goes in my mouth. I have learned since then an important bit of information that might prove helpful: If you think you are going to be sick, eat bananas. They will not make you better, but they taste the same coming up as they do going down. I know that was uncalled for, and I digress. But it is true that what comes out is connected to what goes in. Do you remember the not so ole adage, "garbage in garbage out"? The statement relates to computers and the necessity of putting good data in so that you can get good data out. The principle is the same for us. We must be careful what we allow into our lives because it will have lasting effects. Perhaps this is why Paul said, "Whatsoever things are right and good, honorable and upright, think or dwell on these things" (Philippians 4:8 my paraphrase). Be careful what you watch and think and read, and be careful what you put in your life. A childhood song may make the idea more clear, "Be careful little hands what you do. Oh, be careful little hands what you do. For the Father up above is looking down with love so be careful little hands what you do." Subsequent verses address the eyes and what they see, the mouth and what it says, the feet and where they go, and what the ears hear. The point is clear: Be careful what you allow into your life, not simply because God is watching but because of the lasting effect it will have on your life.

My experience that day did lead me to adjust the rules from, "Won't smoke, won't drink, won't want to." My new rule became: "Won't smoke, won't chew, won't go with girls who do."

Chapter Thirty-Nine

Horsin' Around

During my teenage years, I owned two Red Bone hounds. Red Bone is a breed of dogs that are natural hunting dogs. I spent a lot of time with these dogs training them to hunt raccoons. Coon hunting was an activity that happened at night because raccoons are nocturnal animals. Local farmers were more than willing to allow me to hunt on their property because raccoons, though cute to look at, are a menace.

I have spent many nights and countless hours pursuing this hobby. Sometimes friends would come along, but often I would go alone. Something about the sounds in the night have always been relaxing to me. I would often lie on the hood of my truck and get lost in the stars above while waiting for the dogs to "strike" on a coon's trail.

One of the hazards of coon hunting is that raccoons will sometimes run long distances and swim creeks or rivers before finally climbing into a tree. The hazard is that a dog, in hot pursuit, will go so far and so fast that they are quickly no longer within one's hearing. Therefore, a considerable amount of time can be spent hunting dogs.

There are now new technological gadgets to help, like radio controlled collars and even Global Positioning Systems (GPS) but these were not available to me at the time. Dogs, or at least my dogs, would eventually return to where I released them, but it might be – and most often was – the next morning.

One early morning, I decided to lie down in the bed of my truck and sleep while I waited for the dogs to return. I am not sure how long I was asleep, but in a dreamlike state, I felt a hot burst of air in my face, like breath. The moist, hot blast lured me from my sleep, and as I opened my eyes, a huge shadow loomed over me. And the hot air, yes it was hot breaths of air, were coming from this dark object. In shock, panic, and fear, I screamed as I raised my arms instinctively and struck a horse on the side of the head. The horse wheeled, stumbled, and retreated in fear. The wave of panic gave way to laughter as I realized what had happened.

Fear is often connected with the unknown, isn't it? We have a tendency to fear those things we do not understand or what we do not know. Once the truth emerges, that which was once so frightening can become humorous. The TV show, America's Funniest Videos almost weekly features someone frightened in one second and laughing the next. I am convinced that one of Satan's greatest tactics is to bring fear to our heart, a fear that can paralyze us. The answer is to back up and see the truth. The

Bible says that perfect love casts out all fear (1 John 4:18). When we see and understand the perfect nature of God's love for us and recognize that God has shown this love in such amazing ways we can know we have no reason to fear. Nothing is impossible for God - nothing bigger, nothing stronger. He loves us. We are secure in Him. Life can be scary, but the fear will last only for a moment if we focus on Him and His unchanging love (Romans 8:35-39).

Two hours later, I was back asleep when quietly, the horse returned. This time he simply reached into the back of the truck and bit me on the posterior then ran. This time it was not fear that gripped me, it was pain. But in a short time I was again laughing, and I vowed never to scream in another horses' face.

Chapter Forty

Don't Brake the Truck

My friend Jimmy's dad had a 1948 Chevy truck that he used on their chicken farm. I have told you about my grandparents' chickens, but that was nothing like Jimmy's. Their chicken houses were longer than a football field and home to thousands of chickens. It was quite an operation. Obviously, a farm of this size required tractors and trucks, and among them was this 1948 Chevrolet.

Trucks from the 40's were built like tanks, and this one certainly proved that assessment. Jimmy's dad had newer trucks but none with the character and charm of this one. This truck was an adventure. The starter would not work so we were always careful to park on an incline so we could roll to a start. Now, for some of you, I must tell you that a vehicle with a standard transmission can be started by turning the key, depressing the clutch, putting the vehicle in gear, allowing it to roll and gain speed, then pop the clutch. It usually cranks right up and then continues to move under its own power.

This truck was modified to go because it did not have brakes. In fact, as I recall, it did not even have a brake pedal. Why confuse the driver with a brake pedal if it has no brakes? No pedal kept the driver alert and looking ahead for the proper method of stopping. There seemed to be two, well, three, options that we used. One was to use the gears to slow us down, down-shifting, until we were moving slow enough. (We could also shove it in reverse. This was generally effective.)

On the occasion that we were moving too fast for downshifting and there was not sufficient space to exercise this first method. We just ran into a tree (thus verifying this truck was built like a tank). We would often hit a tree with enough force to deploy an air bag, but there was none. Once again, my childhood experience could have been one of the case studies for yet another safety invention in the automobile world.

I will say farm trucks and tractors with no brakes were more common in those days than you might believe, though. I do not understand why. I did say three methods for stopping, didn't I? The third method of stopping was the same as the second, except when the speed with which we were about to hit a tree prompted us to bail out before impact. Sometimes, at high speeds, we would take our chances out of the truck rather than riding it out.

The unique character of this truck allowed for fun mixed with a little work. Jimmy's older brother would drive on rare occasion while we sat in the back. I say rare because he was known to put the truck on a collision course and abandon ship at the last moment, leaving us to a bruising impact for his own entertainment.

One thing is certain, whoever drove was always alert and looking for a way to stop. I think that is a good practice for life. Life can quickly move in a direction you did not plan, and before you know it, you are out of control. I believe one answer is to have a plan. What will you do when the unexpected happens? Without a plan, you might panic, but with one, you can survive an impact – shaken, but on solid ground.

Having a plan before an accident is the idea behind the saying, "stop, drop and roll." Remember that? We were taught as children if you catch on fire to stop, drop and roll! I heard an older preacher once say that is how we handle the hard and unexpected struggles of life. Stop, drop to your knees, and roll the problem over to God. Not bad advice. Such a plan might keep you from screaming out of control down a hill with no tree in sight. I have been there, too.

Chapter Forty-One

My Tanya

Vacation Bible School is a big deal in most rural churches and a big deal in the lives of the children who attend. I grew up attending VBS, as it was called, and even went two months before I was born. It was always a fun time and a time to discover amazing stories in the Bible and how those stories impact our lives. Even as an adult, I have a special place in my heart for VBS.

It was during VBS that I made the two greatest discoveries of my life. One was that God loved me and demonstrated His love for me by becoming a man, Jesus, and dying on a cross to pay for my sin debt. He rose from the dead as evidence that this sin debt was paid, and through faith in Him, I can be forgiven and restored in right relationship with God. I made that incredible discovery during VBS, and it has changed my life.

The second life-changing discovery I made at VBS was Tanya. My family and hers had known each other for years, but for some reason, my first memory of her was during VBS. She walked in the door, and from the first moment I saw her I was smitten. I still remember it today. I went home that night and asked God if I could have her. Since I was only twelve at the time, I might have asked if I could keep her. I am not sure if it was for that reason, but God did answer my prayer and my childhood sweetheart became my wife about nine years later.

Tanya does not even remember that night; it took a while before she noticed me. But she did! I have often reflected on that time and the simple prayer I offered. As I said, I can't say for sure that God's answer was in response to my prayer, but through the years I have learned to take prayer personally. When I pray and it happens, I praise Him for answering. Now, I am not saying that if you see a girl you like, you should ask God if you can keep her... but it doesn't hurt. Seriously though, we never know what God has in store for us, but spending time with His people in His house opens doors for amazing things. See you in VBS!

Chapter Forty-Two

Love is in the Air

My Tanya lived about five miles from me. That is, if you went by car. Through the woods, our houses were only about one and a half miles apart. So, often I would walk through the woods to see her. It was not like it sounds, there were actually a series of pipe line and high line right of ways that made the walk easy. These right of ways were mowed on a regular basis so they were like a long grass field cut through the woods.

The final leg of the journey, however, was across a large pasture in front of her house. Her dad owned cattle and often they were in the pasture and not really a problem - except for one cow that I believe was demon possessed. She was big and mean and would chase anything that came into that field. Having general knowledge of cattle and particular knowledge of this cow led me to locate the herd before attempting to cross the field. If they were close, I would take the long way around the perimeter.

If they were far enough away, I would climb the fence and cross the pasture.

One day I arrived at the fence line and quickly located the herd. They were gathered at the other end of the pasture so I crossed the fence and started for the other side. When I was about 100 yards from my destination, I heard a pounding on the ground behind me and turned to see this demon possessed cow running hard in my direction. I turned and ran with all the strength I could muster. Just as I reached the fence, she reached me. In a single motion, I put one hand toward the fence post as she launched me into the air. I cleared the fence and the ditch on the other side, landing hard on my back as she slid into the fence.

Now that I think about it, that was my last walk to her house. I got my driver's license shortly after. If I had not been old enough to get my driver's license, I am sure I would have made the journey again, though. Love is a compelling force. Love will motivate us to take great risks. It demands to be shown. It is active. Even in the beginning of our relationship, I was determined to be near her no matter the cost. Today a more seasoned and mature love is even more committed. There is, though, no greater example of love than the love God expressed for you. So desperate to be with you that He paid the ultimate price, and offered the supreme sacrifice of Himself. That is hard to imagine isn't it? The God who created the world wants to have a personal relationship with you. That is why He came and offered His own life as a ransom for us. You see, the Bible says that we are all sinners— none of us are perfect, and the punishment for our sin is death. The good news of God's love is that He came to die in our place to pay our sin debt. That is the story of the Bible - the story of a God who pursues us and calls us to Himself. I often say it is not about a religion it is about a relationship. You can have a relationship with God if you acknowledge your sin, believe that He came in the person of Jesus, died in your place and simply receive Him by asking Him to forgive you and give Him control of your life. A love like that deserves a response.

Chapter Forty-Three

Armadillo on the Loose!

Armadillos are interesting creatures and, given the right set of circumstances, can provide an evening of entertainment. These varmints are common in Louisiana, and it is common knowledge that you can damage your car if you run over them. You see, if you drive over one, not hitting it with your tires, they will jump up and hit the bottom of your car. Now this particular habit most often yields a lethal result. But from time to time, they are just stunned and able to experience a full recovery. As a teenage boy, a friend and I were on our way to town to see a movie. As I was driving, a young armadillo crossed the road in front of me, and I hurried to position my truck over him as he got to the middle of my lane. Predictably, he jumped and hit the bottom of my truck and rolled to the edge of the road. Thinking that he might just be stunned, I stopped and threw him into the back of my truck.

Arriving at the movie, I noticed that he was regaining consciousness and decided to bring him into the theater. My friend bought the tickets and opened the door. I slipped in – holding the "dillo" by the tail. The movie was a horror film so I knew folks were going to enjoy our friend's presence. As the movie became more intense, I released our guest. He began making his way around the theater as the screams from the movie intensified. With every leg he hit, another person would scream and jump up. Before long there was such a commotion the movie was stopped and lights turned on to see what was happening.

Once the armadillo was discovered, my friend and I caught him to the thunderous applause of the theater. We took him out and were given free concessions and free movie tickets. This was a great deal! We left the theater and headed for the local strip.

Pulling behind one of the local burger places, we opened the men's room door, located in the back, and tossed our friend inside. Moments later an elderly man rushed out and told us not to go in. He returned with the manager who discovered an armadillo in the restroom. He seemed bewildered so we offered to catch him and haul him off. He offered us … free food!

By this time we were thinking we should keep him, but opted instead for one last adventure. Off to our favorite teacher's home to stuff our friend in her mailbox. Oh yeah, we backed him in so when she opened the mailbox the next day, he would jump out and get away, and she would be frightened. This, we thought, was a perfect ending to a great night. The only problem was that she was not the first one to open the mailbox. The mailman was, and our friend jumped into his lap! How do I know? Our teacher came to class two days later to tell us the mailman wrecked his Jeep in her driveway ditch. Can you imagine what happened? A mailman minding his own business fumbles through the mail in a routine route, opens the door of the mailbox expecting to retrieve mail (we did leave the flag up) only to be surprised by the prehistoric animal leaping into his lap. I am sorry, I know as an adult I should not feel this way, but I wish I could have seen that. I am taking a risk to share this because it might be against federal law to put an armadillo in a mailbox. Had we thought it through, we might have arranged to get free postage.

Now where do you go with this story? In scripture, animals are often used by God to get our attention. One of my favorite stories as a child was the story of Balaam and the talking donkey from Numbers 22. I am not suggesting that my adventure was used by God in any fashion, but it did get some folks' attention. Sometimes it is necessary to get our attention because ... well, Jesus said it best, "We have ears and do not hear and eyes and do not see." I am grateful that our God loves us enough to use events in life to get our attention, to shake or shock us into seeing and hearing. It is important that we strive to be alert and stay focused to see and hear, but when we become dull or preoccupied do not be surprised if God allows a strategically placed person, event, or even an animal to get our attention.

Chapter Forty-Four

Be Careful What Drives You

I took driver's education after I had received my driver's license. The reason for taking the class at that point was that it reduced our monthly insurance premium. Another advantage is that after receiving your license, you spend a lot of my time running errands for the instructor, who was also one of the football coaches at our school.

There were two other students in our class, and one was a friend of mine named Steve. He also had his license and was taking the course for the same reason. The other girl had never driven a car, and I wondered at the time if she had ever even ridden in one. Steve and I did have to ride with the coach as he instructed her. I do not remember ever driving in driver's education since, and in the coach's mind it was dumb to require us to take the class; after all, we already had our license.

Riding with him and this *real* student driver, however, was an amazing adventure. The instruction was basic and simple since she had no knowledge of where to start. After her class sessions, we would drive to a remote area where the young student driver would get behind the wheel. We started in a church parking lot and then progressed to some rural country roads. She seemed to be catching on, and Steve and I would sit patiently in the back seat as she logged her hours at the wheel. As her confidence increased so did her speed, and we were encouraged that we would actually hit forty miles per hour on the straightaways.

The driver's course proceeded well, that is until we took a new route down a country road a few miles from town. One side of the road was lined with acres and acres of cornfields just about ready for harvesting; on the other side was a river. As we roared along at somewhere around forty miles per hour we came to a sharp ninety degree turn to the right leading to a bridge that crossed over the river.

As we approached the curve, for some reason, the girl driving did not slow down. Granted, forty is not fast but on this turn it was. Just as we got to the critical point, the young student must have frozen because she stiffened her arms and seemed fixed on a spot dead ahead. At that point the coach yelled, as coaches can, "TURN!" She immediately responded, but turned left instead of right, launching us across a ditch into a cornfield. As the car entered the field, we were driving across the rows and at such a speed that as the wheels hit the rows, the car propelled into the air — only to land again on another row. This threw us into the air, striking the top of the car and then back down onto the seat just in time to repeat. Each time we came down, the driver would hit the gas pedal again sending the car skyward yet again. It was the most bizarre thing I have ever experienced; we were tossed about like a rag dolls while the car ripped through the cornfield (in the good ole days, seat belts were not required). I do not know how we finally came to a stop. Steve and I were on the floor in a pile, the girl driving was uncontrollably sobbing in the front seat, and the coach exited the car moving through the cornfield yelling obscenities to the top of his lungs. When he finally returned, he drove the car back over the rows to the road and we started back to town with cornstalks and cornhusks flying into the air. I am not sure what happened to that girl. My guess is that she is still riding the bus, but who knows — maybe she is a driver's education teacher now.

Have you ever felt like you were in the back seat of a car racing through a cornfield? We all know what it is like to be in situations that are out of our control. We are left sobbing uncontrollably, lying bruised and bleeding, flat on the floor, or feel like running or screaming at the top of our lungs. Life does have a way of throwing us curves. One moment all is well and the next we are in a cornfield out of control. God knew that we would face days like that and tells us in those times to turn to Him. Proverbs 3:5-6 says, "Trust in the Lord with all your heart and do not lean on your own understanding. In all your ways acknowledge Him and He will make your path straight."

When life gets out of control, few things make sense. It is in those times of confusion and difficulty that we are to come to Him. He does not promise to make the path easy or short, but he will make it straight and with that straight path provide the strength to walk it. You can't always see God at work when life is out of control, sometimes we are too busy bouncing around in the back seat, but we can trust that He is at work. I like the quote that has been attributed to Charles Haddon Spurgeon, "When you cannot trace the hand of God you can trust His heart."

Afterward

I hope you have enjoyed these stories, and have added a few of your own to the mix. This project began from a desire to share some life lessons with my sons, and leave them with a record of some of my most cherished memories.

The stories in this book come from my childhood, but my discovery that "life is best lived" has continued to guide me in the adult years also.

I will leave you with one story form the next season of my life.

Dr. Carroll D. Mau

Life Is Best Lived ... Really - It Is!

By Dr. Carroll Marr

Chapter One

Sit At Your Own Risk

W hen Tanya and I first married, we rented a small, two bedroom, wood framed house for $50.00 a month. It was a quiet home, with beautiful hardwood floors. It was those hardwood floors that convinced us to rent the home, and they were first thing people noticed when they walked in. Beautiful floors, cheap rent, small honeymoon cottage feel – it was perfect. The landlord was reluctant at first to rent it to me, but we had known each other a long time, and I believe this was a key factor in his willingness to rent it one more time. Our excitement about the prospect of living there changed his mind, so we became newlyweds in our first home.

After moving in, we realized the hardwood floors were just about the only feature of this home that was positive. There were cracks in the walls that allowed cold air in during winter and cool air out in the summer. The house was located adjacent to a hayfield, and when the grass was cut, the mice would leave the field and move in with us. Tanya does not do mice.

As traumatic as this infestation was, the crowning blow – the one that enabled us to bid farewell to our beautiful hardwood floors occurred in the tiny bathroom. You need to know that this framed house sat about four feet off the ground, resting on concrete blocks. One morning, I entered our tiny bathroom, took my seat upon the "throne," and felt the floor move slightly. The movement was so slight, I wondered if I had imagined it. The next movement answered my question because the floor beneath the commode gave way, allowing the commode – with me on it - to fall to ground some four feet below. Strangely, the commode remained upright on the ground with me still perched on top.

The sound of breaking boards and a large crash sent Tanya sprinting to the bathroom and, opening the door, she looked down through the dust to see her husband on the "pot" on the ground. I could lean forward and look out from under the house to see cars passing on the road out front. It was a moving experience.

Needless to say, we moved out, and the owner decided to tear the house down. I pass by the former location of that house every time I return to visit family. It is a part of the hayfield now, but the grass seems greener there.

I do hope you have never experienced anything like that. The resulting trauma from that incident means that the restroom is no longer a place of retreat for me. I want to get in and out as quickly as possible. You may have never had a toilet collapse under you, but I bet you have had experiences that knocked you down, or felt like the "rug was pulled out from underneath you."

It seems that Satan delights in creating situations that trip us up. Temptation, or tragedy – even blessings and comfort can deceive us, and leave us without a firm foundation. In the aftermath of September 11, 2001, I heard author and Pastor Max Lucado say, "when Satan knocked us to our knees, he did not know what we would do once we got there." On our knees, we cry out to a God who is a solid foundation.

The psalmist discovered that, when life pulls the rug from beneath us, if we cry out to God, He will lift us up. Psalm 40:12 declares: "I waited patiently for the Lord; and He inclined to me and heard my cry. He brought me up out of the pit of destruction, out of the miry clay, and He set my feet upon a rock, making my footsteps firm."

Next time the ground gives way beneath you, call out to Him.